THE PATH
to Becoming a
PROVERBS 31
Wife

31 Devotionals
to help you
walk in your
God-given role

Jennifer Rash

The Path to Becoming a Proverbs 31 Wife:
Walking in Your God-Given Role
©2015 Jennifer Rash

ISBN 13: 978-1-937660-92-5
ISBN 10: 1937660923

Published by:
Jennifer Rash

Editor – Hanne Moon, Heritage Press Publications

Cover design – Christine E. Dupre

Interior Design – LisaThomson

"Over the years I've read quite a few studies on Proverbs 31. As a wife of 22 years, I know what it is like to be overwhelmed in marriage by my desire to 'do good' for my husband. Jennifer has written a fresh approach to these holy scriptures. You will be encouraged, challenged, and inspired through her vivid stories as you read each day's devotion. She is so relatable in each chapter that you find yourself cheering you both on as you read. One thing is for sure. We cannot live out our marriages as status quo. We all have room to change and grow. "The Path to Becoming a Proverbs 31 Wife" will do just that–inspire you to change, to grow and to become the wife God has designed you to be."

– Cherie Zack, District Women's Director for the South Carolina District Council of the Assemblies of God and founder of The Imperfect Wives ministry

"Have you ever met someone and you clicked instantaneously? That's how it was for Jennifer and I. We met at a women's conference in 2009. The first thing I noticed was her spirit, she is as humble as they get. It is evident that Jennifer loves God. But she not only has a zeal for God, she has the lifestyle also.

Unfortunately, in today's society there has been an avalanche of brides who no longer take their marriage vows seriously. They love their husbands as long as they have all their wants and needs provided for. They grow tired of comforting and keeping them. They forsake their marriage responsibilities for people, places, and things. They throw *for as long as they both shall live* out the window and substituted it for *as long as it feels good.*

I thank God that Jennifer has been inspired to write this devotional. It is bringing us back to the basics–back to how God intended marriage to be. There is no marital status really required to read this book. It doesn't matter whether you are single, married, separated or divorced. Every person needs to read and receive the message that is placed before you. I am grateful that Jennifer had the courage to remind us of what a marriage is all about. Might I be so bold as to suggest you grab you a cup of coffee or your favorite tea, and buckle up because it all began the moment you said, "I do."

– Sheri Powell, founder of Pausing with God Ministries and Christian author

DEDICATION

This book is dedicated to the number of wives I have counseled and worked with over the past years concerning their marriages and others just like you. You share the most common struggles as wives. Though you may feel like you are the only one, you are not alone. You are not so different after all. Your struggles, your thoughts, your sorrows, your disappointments, your battles, your daily challenges… they are all very much alike. I want to encourage you today—keep moving forward.

Don't quit. You've got this!

Show me the right path, O Lord; point out the road for me to follow.
Psalm 25:4

CONTENTS

Chapter

Introduction: Marriage is Honorable 1

1   I am His Suitable Helper 5

2   I am a Virtuous Wife; a Wife of Valor. 9

3   I am a Devoted Wife. 13

4   I am the Builder of My House. 19

5   I am Full of Purpose as I Build 25

6   I Find Great Satisfaction in Building My Home. 31

7   I am His Encourager 35

8   I Honor and Respect My Husband. 39

9   I am Under the Same Mission as My Husband 45

10   I am Adaptable 51

11   I Follow My Husband's Guidance. 57

12   I Am One With My Husband. 65

13   My Love Story is but a Reflection
of the Greatest Love Story Ever Told 71

14   I Follow Christ's Example in the Way that I Love 77

15   My Marriage is Holy. 83

16   I am a Covenant Keeper. 89

17   I Keep My Heart Clear 95

18   I Handle Conflict Correctly 101

19   I am My Husband's Crown 109

20   I am My Husband's Glory 115

21   I am a Trophy Wife 123

22   I am Strong and Graceful 129

23   I am a Woman Who Fears the Lord 135

24   I am Blessed 141

25   I am a Fruitful Vine Within My House 147

26   I am a Watchman 153

27   My Oil Keeps Burning 159

28   My Lamp Stays Lit 165

29   I Excel 171

30   I am Submitting to the Process 175

31   I Face the Future with a Smile .181

In Closing: Stay on Course 187

INTRODUCTION

Marriage Is Honorable

Let marriage be held in honor (esteemed worthy, precious,
of great price, and especially dear) in all things...

Hebrews 13:4 AMP

Honorable? In what way is my marriage to be honorable? The
Greek word for honorable here is the word timios, which translates
"valuable, costly, honored, esteemed, most precious," and even
"honorable in reputation."

How valuable is your marriage to you? Do you hold your marriage in
high esteem? Our marriages are to be held in honor—in all things
and in all ways. Do you think of your marriage as most precious and
dear? Maybe not. Life has a way of putting pressure on the marriage
relationship, which directly affects the family and the home until
we ourselves no longer have a sense of our own marriage being very
honorable or dear. What do we do in order to bring it back into a
state of preciousness?

Is your marriage honorable before God and before men? Does it honor
God in that it is a reflection of the love of Christ toward His people? Is
it a witness of His unconditional, sacrificial, and enduring love?

By definition, the word "honorable" is defined as "bringing honor and
worthy of respect." How can I contribute to my marriage so that it is
one that brings honor to God?

The Proverbs 31 wife had a marriage that was honorable. Very
often she is referred to as the model wife. Not only did she have
an honorable reputation herself, but because of her character, she
also contributed to the good, honorable reputation of her husband.

Their marriage was honorable before God and also honorable in the community. Today, we are living in a time unlike any other. These are sad times when not only is marriage no longer held in high esteem or looked upon as sacred, but marriage is actually being "redefined" in our culture, something none of us ever thought would happen. God's intentions for instituting the covenant of marriage is being distorted and even perverted. Isn't it even more important today that someone model a marriage that is honorable not only before God, but before the world around us? Will your marriage be that beacon that is shining in the darkness, speaking out to those around you, "God is still very much alive and active, and He is inviting you into a love relationship with Him that looks a lot like *this!*"

There is a much bigger picture here than just being *happy* in our marriages, as we will discover in the next thirty-one days. We will look at what our role is and what it *isn't*. We will learn a lot about ourselves as we look at the characteristics of the Proverbs 31 wife. We will take a very honest look at areas in which we need to grow. We will make fresh new commitments along the way. We will invite the Lord to transform anything that needs transforming.

This thirty-one day devotional is for those who sincerely desire to learn how to become a Proverbs 31 wife, the kind of woman who contributes to a marriage that is honorable in all things, in all ways, and in all respects. I pray that every one of us would grow and develop into the wives that God has called us to be. I pray that our marriages would be full and rich. I speak blessings over your marriage in Jesus' name, that it would not merely survive but thrive, that it would become more than you ever imagined it had the potential to be. I pray that it would be a model to everyone around you, giving them great hope. May it be a marriage your own children and even grandchildren can look to as a blueprint. May a great renewal take place in your own heart from day to day and continue to flourish beyond these thirty-one days.

– JENNIFER RASH

31 Devotional Lessons

The Path to Becoming a Proverbs 31 Wife:

Walking in Your God-Given Role

Cause me to understand Your ways, O Lord! Teach me your paths.

Psalm 25:4 (ISV)

I Am His Suitable Helper

"And the Lord God said, "it is not good that man should be alone;
I will make him a suitable helper comparable to him."
Genesis 2:18 NKJV

I almost chuckle when reading the words, "It is not good that man should be alone." Immediately my thoughts go to the many things that I hear my husband say to me on pretty much a daily basis.

"Jen, where's my keys? Have you seen my wallet? Have my work pants been washed? Will you help me get my lunch together? Did you remember to call...? Hey, did you pay the...? Dinner was great, babe. I love you."

Many of us often wonder, "What in the world would they do without us?"

I remember when my boys were babies. Gary was a wonderful, hands-on dad. He loved to hold them, rock them, feed them, bathe and dress them. The truth was that he was a great daddy and an enormous help to me. I would, however, occasionally find that their little shirts were on backwards, and their shoes were on the wrong feet.

I am sure that there are days when, like myself, you are convinced that the entire household would fall apart without you. Things certainly would not run as smoothly if we were removed from the picture. It's not that our husbands are incapable or incompetent. It just isn't *best* for them to *be alone*. The truth is that they need us!

All joking aside, you yourself know that there are areas in which your husband is very strong, but there are also areas in which he is just not gifted and you fill those gaps. His weaknesses coincidently seem to be your strengths. This is not a coincidence at all.

You have a God-given role to fill. The question is, do you fully understand, appreciate, and embrace the importance of your role as his wife, his helper?

Look at Genesis 2:18 again.

> The LORD God said, "It is not good for the man to be alone. I will make a helper suitable for him." (NIV)

"It is not good" means it is not best, it is not bountiful. These words in Genesis 2 indicate that Adam's strength for all he was called to be and to do was inadequate in itself.

It is vital that you recognize this one thing: your role goes way beyond "helping" with laundry, meals, shopping, finances, running the household, and raising children. Your biblical role is to help him fulfill his God-given purposes—all he is called to be and to do.

A Suitable Helper

Some versions of Genesis 2:18 use the words *helpmate* or *help meet*. The word *help* virtually means "to give assistance or support to." Webster defines *help* like this: "to assist, to lend strength to or means towards effecting a purpose, help forward, to advance by assistance, to aid in completing a design, to enable to surmount."

In this scripture, a *helper* literally translates as "an aid, a backer, an advocate, and a champion" for her husband. Most translations use the words "a suitable helper."

> **Suitable** – precisely adapted to a particular situation, need, or circumstance; fitting.

Do you believe that you were made for him? Your makeup, the way you are wired, your strengths, are fitting to his particular needs and his set of circumstances. There is no one more fitting than you. You are suitable or just right for him!

Your role is to compliment him. You are his counterpart. In other words, you are part of him, called alongside him to be a help, a backer, and an advocate, and the one who helps him to fulfill his God-given purposes.

What do I believe my husband's God given purposes are?

_____

_____

_____

_____

How can I lend strength towards effecting those purposes?

_____

_____

_____

_____

How can I support, aid, back, and encourage the fulfillment of those things?

_____

_____

_____

_____

Prayer

Lord, today I understand, appreciate, and embrace my God-given and ordained role as my husband's suitable helper. It is my desire that he become all that You have called him to be and accomplish all that You have called him to do. Show me how I can lend strength toward effecting those purposes. Reveal to me the ways that I might help him advance and move forward in every way. Lord, You know that I've got his back! I am in his corner. Help me, in spite of all of my imperfections and shortcomings, truly become a champion for my husband and the wife that You have called me to be.

PERSONAL REFLECTIONS

_____

_____

_____

_____

_____

_____

_____

_____

_____

_____

I Am a Virtuous Wife, a Wife of Valor

Who can find a virtuous wife? For her worth is far above rubies. The heart of her husband safely trusts her; so he will have no lack of gain.

Proverbs 31:10-11 (NKJV)

What is a **virtuous** wife and why is she so valuable?

A wife who is virtuous is one who lives according to high moral standards and goals. She is pure, innocent, morally admirable, and excellent. No wonder he can trust her!

The Message puts it like this: "Her husband trusts her without reserve, and never has reason to regret it."

The AMPC says, "Her husband trusts in her confidently and relies on and believes in her securely…"

Now that kind of trust is a valuable thing, isn't it? There is no material object, however costly, that can compare. The CEV says that this kind of wife is the "most precious treasure a man can find."

Many versions of Proverbs 31 use another word in place of virtuous. It is the word valor. – "Who can find a wife of valor…"

Valor is defined here as "great courage in the face of danger or battle, strength of mind or spirit that enables a person to encounter adversity with firmness or personal bravery."

Not only is she worthy of his confidence and trust, but this wife is his calm and steady in every trial, storm, attack, and battle they face together in life. She is anchored in her faith and relationship with Christ. She doesn't fall apart when trouble comes their way. She is strong. She is solid. Whether in sickness or health, good times or bad, joy or sorrow, in prosperous times and when things are lean, she is steady. She navigates the course of their journey together with great courage rather than fear. She possesses an inner strength of mind and spirit that causes her to face whatever comes their way like a real champ. He can indeed rely on her to be strong when the pressures of life are real.

These characteristics are certainly admirable to say the least. What a benefit and gain it is to find a virtuous wife, a wife of valor.

In what ways do I exhibit these characteristics in my life as a wife?

———————————————————————————————

———————————————————————————————

———————————————————————————————

———————————————————————————————

In what ways do I need to grow concerning virtue and valor?

———————————————————————————————

———————————————————————————————

———————————————————————————————

How do I respond in daily battles, times of stress and pressure, in the midst of great challenges, when faced with adversity and even calamity? Do I have strength of mind and spirit, or do I crash and sink?

———————————————————————————————

_____

_____

_____

Can he count on me to be the partner that he can lean on?

_____

_____

_____

_____

Prayer

Lord, I strive to live my life morally and in a way that pleases You. I want to be the kind of wife that my husband can confidently trust and rely on. Help me to be the mature counterpart that lends strength to him through every season of our lives together. Make me a wife of virtue and a wife of valor.

PERSONAL REFLECTIONS

_____

_____

_____

_____

_____

_____

_____

_____

_____

_____

_____

_____

_____

_____

_____

_____

_____

_____

_____

_____

_____

_____

_____

_____

_____

_____

_____

_____

Day 3

I Am a Devoted Wife

*She does him **good** and not evil all the days of her life.*
Proverbs 31:12 (NASB)

Of course she does him good, right? What kind of wife would do evil to her own husband? Maybe we should explore a couple of key words in this verse...

The word good is the Hebrew word *tôv* and it means "to be of benefit, to be kind, pleasant, and agreeable." Once again we are talking about one's character and disposition.

Let's first consider defining the word "kind." I had an interesting phone conversation with a wife who had become very wounded from the act of exchanging unkind words with her husband over a long period of time. It started out as shooting smart remarks at each other and returning insult for insult. It should have stopped after that first bad day. It should have ended with apologies and the resolve to stop. Instead, it became a regular thing. It turned into a bad habit. It went on and on for years. They continued to take jabs at each other daily. The words cut. The remarks hurt. It was a downward spiral that led to a relationship in need of a lot of repair.

If we look ahead to verse 27 of Proverbs 31, we read, "She opens her mouth with wisdom, and on her tongue is the law of kindness." Hmm. We will come back to that later...

I suppose one could be kind or even unkind in many ways—through words or actions. What might cause someone to be unkind, unpleasant, or just plain disagreeable? Sometimes this kind of behavior can be rooted in hurt, anger, unforgiveness, bitterness, or resentment. We must continually do a heart check so that we do not walk through life with unresolved issues within. Women must become good releasers. When offense comes through our own husband's or another's words or actions, we must know how to release the offense. We must not hold onto these negative thoughts and emotions, or they will eventually erupt.

A virtuous wife, a wife of valor, does not hold onto offense but releases it. She doesn't take poison in; therefore, what comes out of her is sweet rather than bitter.

Am I holding onto something in my heart? Do I have unresolved hurt, anger, unforgiveness, bitterness or resentment within me?

_____

_____

_____

_____

Am I kind, pleasant and agreeable?

_____

_____

_____

Prayer #1

Lord, help me to become good at releasing negative thoughts and feelings before they take root and get in the driver's seat of my every relationship, especially my relationship with my husband. Lord, I release every hurt and offense of the past to you now, in Jesus' name. Christ the Healer, come and heal every place. Go to and through each place that has been wounded. Christ the Forgiver who lives in me, release forgiveness through me to every offender of my heart. From this day forward, cause me to immediately recognize any poison coming my way and boldly exclaim, "No! I am not taking that in." Help me to keep my heart free and clear. Help me to walk in peace with You and with my husband.

Sometimes unkind, unpleasant, and disagreeable behavior can be the byproduct of a tired and ornery person.

Am I getting enough rest?

_____

_____

_____

_____

Am I eating right?

_____

_____

_____

_____

Do I take good care of myself?

_____

_____

_____

_____

Are these things affecting my overall personality and disposition?

_____

_____

_____

_____

Prayer #2

Lord, teach me to balance my life in such a way that I am healthy physically, mentally, emotionally, and spiritually, as one area always affects the others. Lord, remind me daily to stay in communion and fellowship with You. When I have spent time with You, my other relationships reap the benefits. I have the right perspective, no matter what is happening all around me. I walk in peace. My desire is to first and foremost please You. Good things flow out of this place in my heart. I want to be the kind of wife who does my husband good and not evil all the days of my life. I realize that "all the days of my life" means continually. "All the days of my life" means that I am in this thing for the long haul. I am a committed woman. I am a devoted wife!

How have I been good to my husband?

_____

_____

_____

_____

In what ways am I falling short and how can I make a fresh commitment?

_____

_____

_____

_____

How can I renew my devotion to him and my commitment to the things that are in his best interest and for his good?

_____

_____

_____

_____

Prayer #3: My own heartfelt prayer…

_____

_____

_____

_____

PERSONAL REFLECTIONS

_____

_____

_____

_____

_____

_____

Day 4

I Am the Builder Of My House

She does him good and not **evil** *all the days of her life.*
Proverbs 31:12 (NASB)

Continuing with Proverbs 31:12 today, let's look at the word "evil." Again the question arises, "No wife would intentionally do evil to her husband, right?"

The word "evil" here is the Hebrew word *ra* (masculine form) or *râ âh* (feminine form). Interestingly enough, it translates "unkind, disagreeable, malignant, and vicious in disposition." It can mean "adversity, affliction, bad, calamity, displeasure, distress, grief, harm, hurt, injury, misery, sorrow, trouble, vex, wrong, mischief, wicked or evil ethically in thoughts or actions."

A virtuous wife has her husband's best interests and good in mind. She is not self-seeking. She is never spiteful. She doesn't set out to manipulate and control him in any way. She does not withhold affection as a means of punishment when she does not get her way. She is not contentious. After all, how could a man benefit or gain anything living in that kind of atmosphere?

No "good" will result from living in a home with a wife who walks in this kind of disposition and behavior.

Proverbs 25:24 says, "It is better to dwell in the corner of the housetop than to share a house with a disagreeing, quarrelsome, and scolding woman." (AMP)

Proverbs 21:19 says, "It is better to dwell in a desert land than with a contentious woman and with vexation." (AMP)

Vexation – annoyance: anger produced by some annoying irritation

The Amplified version puts it like this; "It is better to dwell in a corner of the housetop [on the flat oriental roof, exposed to all kinds of weather] than in a house shared with a nagging, quarrelsome, and faultfinding woman." – Proverbs 25:24

And Proverbs 27:15-16 says, "A constant dripping on a day of steady rain and a contentious (quarrelsome) woman are alike; whoever attempts to restrain her (criticism) might as well try to stop the wind, and grasps oil with his right hand." (AMP)

Wow! A malignant, vicious or unethical woman will surely bring grief and sorrow to her husband! It is also pretty clear how an unrestrained, disagreeing, quarrelsome, scolding, nagging, and fault-finding wife will make a home a miserable place.

Proverbs 14:1 says, "A wise woman builds her house; but a foolish woman tears hers down with her own hands." (NASB)

The words "tear down" translate to "pull down or in pieces, break and destroy, ruin, and overthrow."

Truly, it's a foolish woman who would do such a thing. Continuing in any of the behavior we have just outlined would be foolish. We have been called to build our homes! One of our *greatest* roles is that of building our homes. The truth is that we have been anointed to do that very thing. It is in us! I don't know about you, but I want to be the woman that Proverbs 14:1 describes as wise.

A wise woman builds her house; but a foolish woman tears hers down with her own hands. (Proverbs 14:1 NASB)

The word "build" is the Hebrew word *bânâh* and it means "to build, make, repair, set (up)."

I believe that there is great contentment and satisfaction to be found in the building of our homes. In order for a woman to become a good builder of her home, it is important for her to know what her role *is* and what her role *isn't*. It is just as important to learn what not to do as it is to learn what to do.

Building your home requires action. Building is a process. Building takes effort and work. It is an ongoing job or role. In a sense, building our homes *is* a job.

Today, begin to break wrong habits and set up or build new habits! Be willing. Adapt yourself. Build your home. Build your husband. Be full of purpose in what you are doing as you build! Be that wise woman who builds her house!

Have I been operating in any of these destructive behaviors or patterns?

_____

_____

_____

_____

What are some ways that I have been tearing down or tearing apart my own home with my own hands?

_____

_____

_____

What are some ways that I can build and even repair my home?

_____

_____

_____

Prayer

Lord, make me a wise woman who builds her house. In no way do I want to tear down my own house with my own hands, my own words, or my own behavior. I desire to be kind, pleasant, and agreeable. I desire that our home be the place my husband cannot wait to return to, a home filled with love and peace, a safe place where he can always find comfort and encouragement. Let it be a haven after a long, difficult day. Let it be a welcoming, sweet atmosphere when he has encountered an unkind world. Let it be a place of healing when someone out there has taken a bite out of him. Oh, that our home would be the place where all tension melts to the ground as soon as he steps through the door because he is home sweet home!

PERSONAL REFLECTIONS

_____

_____

_____

_____

_____

_____

_____

_____

_____

_____

_____

_____

_____

_____

_____

_____

_____

_____

_____

_____

_____

_____

_____

_____

_____

_____

_____

_____

_____

Day 5

I Am Full of Purpose
As I Build

She seeks wool and flax, and willingly works with her hands. She is like the merchant ships, she brings her food from afar. She also rises while it is yet night, and provides food for her household, and a portion for her maidservants. She considers a field and buys it; from her profits she plants a vineyard. She girds herself with strength, and strengthens her arms. She perceives that her merchandise is good, and her lamp does not go out by night. She stretches out her hands to the distaff, and her hand holds the spindle.

She extends her hand to the poor, yes, she reaches out her hands to the needy. She is not afraid of snow for her household, for all her household is clothed with scarlet. She makes tapestry for herself; her clothing is fine linen and purple. Her husband is known in the gates, when he sits among the elders of the land. She makes linen garments and sells them, and supplies sashes for the merchants. Strength and honor are her clothing; she shall rejoice in time to come.

She opens her mouth with wisdom, and on her tongue is the law of kindness. She watches over the ways of her household, and does not eat the bread of idleness. Her children rise up and call her blessed; her husband also, and he praises her: "Many daughters have done well, but you excel them all."

Charm is deceitful and beauty is passing, but a woman who fears the Lord, she shall be praised. Give her of the fruit of her hands, and let her own works praise her in the gates.

Proverbs 31:13-31 (NKJV)

Here in verses 13-31, we see the virtuous wife diligently building her home. She is not idle. No, in fact, she is very productive. She is completely dedicated to her tasks at hand, her responsibilities, and the activities of her household. She is a good manager and a good steward of all that the Lord has given her. She, not her husband, manages the household.

This woman is full of purpose as she builds. She works joyfully with her hands. She definitely senses the value and worth of her work. The Proverbs 31 wife is up before dawn and is in no hurry to call it quits.

Apparently she understands that building is like sowing and planting. She is investing in the lives of her husband and children. A day is coming when she will see the fruit of her labor, so she pours herself out. She girds herself with strength and strengthens her arms, according to verse 17. She carries herself with strength, honor and dignity. She energetically takes care of the family's needs. They are blessed because of her.

I like the way the Amplified version puts verses 15-17:

> She rises while it is yet night and gets [spiritual] food for her household and assigns her maids their tasks. (v 15)

She is not only looking after her family's physical needs, but she is also dedicated to their spiritual well-being. She is up while everyone else is still asleep, not doing chores, but in the Word of God and in prayer. She stays in communion with the Lord. She knows Him and she hears Him. This woman has a deep commitment to her husband and children because she first has a deep commitment to her God. And look at the next verse.

> She considers a [new] field before she buys or accepts it [expanding prudently and not courting neglect of her present duties by assuming other duties]; with her savings [of time and strength] she plants fruitful vines in her vineyard. (v 16)

This woman has her priorities in order. The verse says that she does not neglect her present duties by assuming other duties. She has made her husband and her children, the building of her home, the top priority. She knows how to keep the main things, the main thing. This woman doesn't let anything crowd out the things that are of most importance to her. She places nothing or no one before her husband and children. Nothing will take their place in her heart or with her time. She doesn't allow things to get out of balance. She remains focused.

> She girds herself with strength [spiritual, mental, and physical fitness for her God-given task] and makes her arms strong and firm. (v 17)

The Proverbs 31 wife takes care of herself so that she can continue being the best wife that she can be. She knows that if she is strong spiritually, mentally, and physically, she can best serve God and her household.

Do I sense a great calling in my life in the building of my home?

_____

_____

_____

_____

Is there anything in my life that has caused me to compromise or place my husband and the building of our home in second place to my other activities?

_____

_____

_____

_____

Have I taken on too much outside of my home?

_____

_____

_____

_____

Where and how can I find balance and take back control of the hours of my life in order to keep my priorities aligned?

_____

_____

_____

_____

Does my husband know that he is my priority?

_____

_____

_____

_____

Prayer

Lord, fill me with a great sense of purpose in all that I do as the builder of my home. The building of my home is entirely significant. Help me to be a good manager and steward of all that You have given me. Teach me how to strike a healthy balance in all that I am doing inside and outside of my home. Show me where I need to make adjustments. My sincere desire is to have a healthy marriage and a healthy home.

PERSONAL REFLECTIONS

Day 6

I Find Great Satisfaction in the Building of My Home

She looks well on how things go in her household, and the bread of idleness (gossip, discontent, and self-pity) she will not eat.

Proverbs 31:27 AMP

The Proverbs 31 wife finds great satisfaction in her role of being a wife and in the activities involved in building her home. She doesn't view her activities as menial. She isn't feeling sorry for herself. After all, building is hard work, but her attitude isn't that of "Woe is me!" Even when she doesn't see immediate rewards, she is sure that she is blessed and most fortunate. There is a great sense of purpose and, therefore, value in all that she does. She feels privileged and most thankful.

Unlike the woman who begins to believe that the grass must be greener on the other side of the fence, she knows the importance of nurturing the grass in the field that the Lord has given to her.

Building her home and walking in her God-given role has caused her to feel greatly fulfilled in a very real way.

She doesn't have time to sink into a state of idleness which often leads a woman to becoming a busy-body, always concerned about everyone else's business instead of her own. She doesn't go there. She refuses to even keep company with this type. Determined not to take in negative thoughts and emotions, she has grown into a mature and seasoned woman, a woman who is content. After all, godly contentment is great gain.

> [And it is, indeed, a source of immense profit, for] godliness accompanied with contentment (that contentment which is a sense of inward sufficiency) is great and abundant gain. (1 Timothy 6:6-11 AMP)

> **Contentment** – a state of happiness and satisfaction.

Easton's Bible Dictionary defines contentment here as "a state of mind in which one's desires are confined to his lot, whatever it may be."

Albert Barnes says that contentment is "a state of mind, a calm and satisfied feeling, a freedom from murmuring and complaining, a peace of mind and true riches."

Godliness and contentment are companions. These two characteristics walk together hand in hand. Because the Proverbs 31 wife has pursued godliness, she experiences real contentment in her life. According to verse 27, she looks upon her activities and role as a wife and feels good about it. She also has a positive outlook about the future.

> Strength and dignity are her clothing and her position is strong and secure; she rejoices over the future [the latter day or time to come, knowing that she and her family are in readiness for it]! (Proverbs 31:25 AMP)

She has given her life to the Lord and serving Him in the building of her home. Her mind and heart are set on the right things. Her perspective is the Lord's perspective. She is not anxious about anything but looks forward to the future with joy. She always faces tomorrow with a smile.

Do I feel good about how things are going in my household? If not, what could be going better?

_____

_____

_____

_____

On a scale of 1 to 10, how content am I at this present time?

_____

_____

_____

_____

What are the things that cause me to feel the greatest sense of satisfaction in my life right now and why?

_____

_____

_____

_____

Do I find great satisfaction in the fulfilling of my role as a wife and in the activities involved in building my home? Why or why not?

_____

_____

_____

_____

Do I need freedom from murmuring and complaining?

_____

_____

_____

_____

Prayer

Lord, fill me with a great sense of fulfillment in the building of my home. Show me how to build well. Place in my heart a growing love for sowing and planting in the field of my marriage. Create in me a contentment, an inner peace, and a real satisfaction in knowing that I am building according to Your plan. Lord, as I build my home, I ask that You build me. In Jesus' name. Amen.

PERSONAL REFLECTIONS

_____

_____

_____

_____

_____

_____

_____

_____

Day 7

I Am His Encourager

She comforts, encourages, and does him only good
as long as there is life within her.
Proverbs 31:12 AMP

Not only do I build my house, but I build my man. I am his encourager. Is he low? Is he feeling down? Comfort him and lift him up! The word encourage comes from the old French word *encoragier*, meaning "to make strong, hearten."

> **Encourage** – to give support, confidence and hope to. Uplift, cheer, promote, nurture and strengthen.

Just as one can either build or tear down one's home by their own hands, one can also build or tear down their own husband by their own hands. We can be either a great source of encouragement or discouragement. Being a discourager to our husband is a dangerous thing.

In order to walk in their own role as our husbands, the leaders and high priests of our homes (along with many other things), they must have strength, courage, grit, and bravery! They must possess the quality of mind and spirit that enables them to face tough challenges, difficulty, danger, fear, and pain. We had better not tear down our husband's spirit. Mental and moral strength and confidence is vital if he is ever going to be the kind of man that you want him to be.

It is never a good idea to tear your husband down.

When it comes to the word discourage, here is what we need to know. The prefix "dis" means "to turn away from." Therefore the word *discourage* means to turn away from courage. When our husbands are navigating through the difficulties of life, we had better be in their corner rooting for them. We had better be their cheerleader chanting the words, "You can do it. You got this. You are the man!"

Remember, one of our most important roles by design is to help them be all that God has called them to be and to do. We are to help them fulfill their God-given purposes. When they are facing disappointments, we best be speaking encouraging, life-giving words. As you can guess by our last word study, the word *disappointment*, having the same prefix as discouragement, means "to turn away from one's appointment."

There are things that your husband will face that will cause him to want to give up, quit, drop out, throw up his hands, and walk away from the things that God has purposed him to fulfill. These are the days when he needs you to be that comforting, encouraging voice that he comes home to. You are the woman who believes in him and supports him no matter what.

How do I encourage my husband? I encourage him with my words.

> She opens her mouth in skillful and godly wisdom and on her tongue is the law of kindness [giving counsel and instruction]. (Proverbs 31:26 AMP)

> When she speaks she has something worthwhile to say and she says it kindly. (Proverbs 31:26 MSG)

The Proverb's 31 wife has developed a skill of knowing just what to say. She thinks before she speaks. Her words are wise words. Her tongue isn't sharp. Her words aren't cutting and they are kind. Her words have the power to comfort, soothe, and heal. Often her words reassure. Her words are a source of encouragement and strength. With her support, he can accomplish anything!

He never discounts what she has to say because he has come to value her input and many times asks for her advice and counsel. She is his godly wife, full of wisdom and discernment. She is for him and not against him. She's got his back. She is his biggest fan.

Her great outlook about the present *and* the days ahead lends confidence to him. And her positive attitude in life helps him to also face the future with hope and joy.

Have my words been used to encourage or discourage, build up or tear down?

_____

_____

_____

_____

What does my husband need to hear from me today?

> *"I appreciate you."*
> *"Thank you, for all that you do."*
> *"You are a good provider."*
> *"You take good care of us."*

_____

_____

_____

_____

Prayer

Lord, I choose to build up my husband and be a great source of encouragement to him. Use me, Lord, to lend mental and moral strength to him daily. Give me wise words. Let my words comfort, soothe, and heal. Speak to me, Lord, about my husband's needs in this area. Let my attitude be one that creates a positive atmosphere rather than one that pulls him down. Help me to build this man's spirit and not to break it. I desire for my husband to become all that You have created him to be. Then, and only then, will he become all that I truly need him to be. Teach me, Lord, that I may use the power of my words for his good as long as there is life within me.

Personal Reflections

_____

_____

_____

_____

_____

_____

_____

_____

_____

_____

_____

_____

_____

_____

I Honor and Respect My Husband

Her husband is respected at the gates,
where he takes his seat among the elders of the land.

Proverbs 31:23 (NIV)

A godly wife will give her husband a good reputation among the public world. In the community, he will be well respected.

A wife's moral conduct will reflect upon her husband's reputation as well as hers. Verse 25 tells us that the Proverbs 31 wife carries herself with strength and dignity. Her strength, honor, and dignity bring honor to his reputation as well as to hers. After all, the woman takes the man's last name when she weds. She no longer goes by her maiden name. In a very real way, she now represents the good family name that she has married into. Have you ever thought about that? When we become Christians, we say that we have taken on the name of Christ. We represent Christ to the world around us. We want to honor His name and be a good testimony before others. In a similar way, we have taken our husband's name and bring either honor or dishonor to him.

Not only will your personal conduct reflect on his reputation, but the way you speak about him to others will either honor him or dishonor him.

I don't know about you, but I really hate to hear someone speaking negatively about their spouse. What is even more unbecoming is when someone puts down and criticizes their spouse right in front of them. Have you ever heard a wife belittle her husband in front of people? It is utter disrespect and only causes people to look poorly upon the one who is doing the dishonoring.

Sure, your husband has flaws. Everyone's spouse has flaws. We all have flaws. I have flaws. You have flaws. But when it comes to your husband's flaws, you just don't need to tell it. If you are really having a struggle with one of his character flaws (and at some point you will), pour your heart out to the Lord. He is the only one who has the power to change it. The Holy Spirit is the only one who can transform a heart and a life. The only way any good can come out of you sharing your husband's flaws, faults, shortcomings, weaknesses, and failures is when you have shared them with Christ in prayer. The Lord, who is still working on you, will continue to work on your husband.

It is your job as his wife to cover his weaknesses. I don't mean "cover up," but I am talking about a cover of protection. Honor him privately and always honor him publically. Never speak negatively about your husband to others. Make that man look better than he really is. Not only do you build him up by speaking uplifting and encouraging words *to* him, but you build him up by speaking uplifting and encouraging words *about* him.

If you have demonstrated before others that you do not respect him, others will not respect him either.

It is important for us to understand just what our role is and just what our role isn't. Many times, wives who are mothers spend much time training, disciplining, and correcting children. Because of this, wives have a tendency to fall into the poor habit of talking to their husbands in the same manner that they talk to their children. Have you ever heard a wife talk to her husband like he was a little boy? Have you ever seen a wife treat her husband like a child? This gives the appearance that she does not believe that her husband is capable of doing anything right. One would think that she does not have a bit of confidence in him.

Unfortunately, this kind of behavior will cause others to doubt his capabilities as well. You are not your husband's mother. You are his wife. These two roles look very different. You are to respect him as another competent adult. You are to respect him as a man. You must not talk down to him, chide him, humiliate him, or emasculate him— not in private and certainly not in public.

Never speak poorly about your husband. Only speak highly of him. If you will honor him and respect him both privately and publically, you will increase his influence in the world around him. The Proverbs 31 wife was influential in her husband's success because she honored and respected him.

In Ephesians 5:33, Paul tells men that they are to love their wives. However, we do not find him also telling women that they are to love their husbands. Instead he tells them that they are to "respect" their husbands. It seems that women do not have difficulty loving like Christ loves, making any sacrifices necessary. Women love and they love deeply. Respect, on the other hand, is the area that apparently needed to be addressed. What about you today? Are you strong in the area of demonstrating sacrificial love toward your husband, yet weak in demonstrating respect?

_____

_____

_____

How can I demonstrate honor and respect toward my husband?

_____

_____

_____

_____

Where have I fallen short in this area?

_____

_____

_____

_____

What fresh commitments do I need to make today?

_____

_____

_____

_____

Do I pray for my husband daily?

_____

_____

_____

_____

Prayer

Lord, thank you for the gift You have given me in my husband.
Forgive me, Lord, for any ways in which I have dishonored or
disrespected him in private and in public. I repent for any and every
time that I have spoken negatively about my husband. Help me to
focus on his many strengths rather than his few shortcomings. Help me
to see him through Your eyes, for you see the finished product. Thank
You for moving and working in his life. Continue to shape and mold
him into the man You created him to be. Remind me daily, Lord, to
pray for my husband.

PERSONAL REFLECTIONS

_____

_____

_____

_____

_____

_____

_____

_____

_____

_____

_____

_____

_____

_____

_____

_____

_____

_____

_____

_____

_____

_____

Day 9

I Am Under the Same Mission As My Husband

*In like manner, you married women, **be submissive** to your own husbands [**subordinate yourselves as being secondary to and dependent on them**, and **adapt yourselves to them**], so that even if any do not obey the Word [of God], they may be won over not by discussion but by the [godly] lives of their wives, when they observe the pure and modest way in which you conduct yourselves, together with your reverence [for your husband; **you are to feel for him all that reverence includes: to respect, defer to, revere him—to honor, esteem, appreciate, prize, and, in the human sense, to adore him, that is, to admire, praise, be devoted to, deeply love, and enjoy your husband**].*

1 Peter 3:1-2 (AMP)

I have bolded a few words and terms in the above verses to make some related points. I encourage you to go back and read these verses again and underline words that have spoken to you in some way. Some of these words really reinforce our last devotional on honor and respect. I have been meditating on the words...

- Appreciate
- Prize
- Adore
- Admire
- Enjoy

These are actually some very beautiful verses of scripture. The main topic in this passage is that of submission. Submission is not a dirty word that we as woman should be offended by. The world has given the word submission its negative connotation because it has not understood it.

In this passage, the first words that we see as related to submission are "subordinate yourselves as being secondary to and dependent upon..." This idea of being secondary really gets some women riled up! After all, our society says that women should be equal, and a women can do anything that a man can do, right? Well, no. That is not right when it comes to their God-ordained roles.

The role of a wife and the role of a husband are quite different. I am so glad that I don't have to try to be and do everything that my husband is and does. That would wear me out!

The truth is that, when you get married, it's no longer all about you anymore. You no longer live for only you. You no longer put yourself first. We all understand that but "to subordinate oneself as being secondary" actually has more to do with rank. It means lower in rank and position. It means to place yourself under authority. We know from scripture that the husband's role is to be the head of the union—the head of his household or family. This is his position or rank according to God. We place ourselves under his authority.

Authority gives one *the freedom to decide and the right to act without any hindrance.* The concept of authority is to have "the power, ability, or capability to complete an action."

Well, if that's the case, Lord, help my husband to walk in his authority for the good of my family, and don't let me hinder or get in the way of that!

Looking again at the words "subordinate oneself as being secondary and **dependent on**," let's take a minute and consider the idea of being dependent on our husbands. Being dependent on my husband doesn't mean that I cannot do anything without him because I am so weak and incapable. My goodness, if that were the case, he would have never been attracted to me in the first place. I don't know anyone who wants to spend the rest of their life with a weak and incapable partner. No, our Proverbs 31 model wife is even described as *capable*, but we'll come back to that thought later...

If you can depend on someone, you can trust and rely on them. You can count on them for help and support. They are someone you can lean on when you need to. I am so thankful that my husband is the one person who I can truly depend on. I don't know about you, but I need to be able to depend on someone. There are things that my husband depends on and relies on me for, and there are definitely things that I depend on him for. I put him first, I depend on him, and I'm not ashamed to say it!

The next words that we see in these verses as being related to submission are "adapt yourselves." Adapt means "to become adjusted to new conditions or to make suitable for a new use or purpose."

This falls right in line with our role as our husband's "suitable helper," the one who helps him to fulfill his God-given purpose. When we marry, we become one with our husband. We are on a journey together going in the same direction, with the same focus, working together toward the same goals and mission. In fact, submission actually means "to be under the same mission."

Submission – to be under the same mission

The prefix *sub-* means "to be under." Therefore, submission means to be under one and the same mission. A mission, by the way, is a calling or an important assignment.

Not only do I help my husband fulfill his God-ordained calling and purpose, but I have become one with him in his mission. I am not on one mission and he on another. Our lives have been joined. I have come under a common mission. We are doing life together. God has a plan and purpose for us as one.

Do I put my husband first, even before myself? Does my husband know that he is the number one person in my life?

_____

_____

_____

_____

Am I hindering my husband in any way from operating in his God-given authority in our home?

_____

_____

_____

_____

Do I realize just how much I really do depend on him?

_____

_____

_____

_____

Do I appreciate him? Do I consider him a prize?

_____

_____

_____

_____

What is our calling as a married couple? What is our common mission?

_____

_____

_____

_____

Prayer

Lord, thank you for giving me a covering of safety under my husband's headship. I willingly place myself under his leadership in our marriage and in our home. Help him to be the best leader that he can be. Help me not to hinder him in any way as he seeks to be that leader and as he functions in his God-ordained role. As I consider all the ways that I can depend on him, I am filled with a new appreciation. Cause me to develop an even deeper love and adoration for my husband. You have always had a plan and a purpose for me, Lord. You are a good God. But I recognize, even more today, that you have a plan and a purpose for us together as a married couple. You have a mission for us as one.

PERSONAL REFLECTIONS

_____

_____

_____

_____

_____

_____

_____

_____

_____

_____

_____

_____

_____

_____

_____

_____

_____

_____

_____

_____

_____

_____

_____

_____

_____

_____

Day 10

I Am Adaptable

*In like manner, you married women, be submissive to your own
husbands [subordinate yourselves as being secondary to and dependent
on them, and **adapt yourselves** to them], so that even if any do not
obey the Word [of God], they may be won over not by discussion but
by the [godly] lives of their wives.*

1 Peter 3:1 (AMPC)

Submit – put yourself under, **adapt yourselves**, coming under the
"cover" of your husband who is under the cover of Jesus Christ.

While we have gained a better understanding of what it means to
willingly place ourselves under our husband's covering of authority as
we come under a common mission, today I want to look closer at the
words "adapt yourself." Let us consider what it means to adapt. Having
the ability to adapt is vital to growth and forward movement in all
areas of our lives.

Adapt – to become adjusted to new conditions or to make
suitable for a new use or purpose, to modify, adjust or readjust,
rework or make it work, acclimate oneself, to come to terms
with, to get one's bearings, to find one's feet.

Hmm. Is adapting necessary in married life?

On your wedding day, you made a vow that sounded something like this:

> I,_____, *take thee,_____,*
> *to be my wedded husband, to have and to hold from this day*
> *forward, for better or for worse, for richer or for poorer, in*
> *sickness and in health, to love, cherish, and to obey, till death do*
> *us part, according to God's holy ordinance.*

For better or for worse, for richer or for poorer, in sickness or in health speaks to me about the need to adapt to whatever circumstances we might find ourselves in as a married couple. Can you be just as committed and passionate in difficult times as you are in the happy, on-top-of-the-world times? Can you be just as committed and loving in the season of lack as you are in the season of sufficiency? Can you be just as committed and faithful in the hour of sickness as you are in the days of health?

I have never met anyone whose life has always remained calm and comfortable all the time. Most of us have, at one time or another, been thrown into a sudden change. We have found ourselves in circumstances that we didn't ask for and we certainly never dreamed or imagined we would be in. This is true in a marriage and it is certainly true of life. The Lord desires that we, as a married couple, stay on top no matter what winds of change blow into our lives. Our ability to adapt is vital to our survival and vitality. We must become women who can quickly and easily become adjusted to new conditions, women who are resilient.

This is one of those important things that sets our marriages apart from those that didn't make it. For years, studies have shown that over half of marriages end in divorce both in and out of the church. That's over half among non-Christians and Christians alike. This should not be true! Nevertheless, it is. We, as born again, Spirit-filled believers are overcomers, more than conquerors—right?

I am intrigued when reading about nature, God's creation. Many plants and animals, for example, adapt out of a need to survive because of changing environments and even the threat of predators. They have learned to cope with extreme and harsh temperatures, withstand hostile conditions, conquer relentless forces, and protect themselves from predators without sustaining one scratch or injury.

There are some animals that can store water and even food within their own bodies for times when water and food will be scarce. Others grow thick coats of fur in order to keep warm in the winter season and shed these same coats when the weather starts to warm up. There are certain species of fish that can live in the freezing arctic waters where others cannot. These particular fish possess a special protein which allows their cells to continue with the life cycle even under those extreme conditions.

In the tropical regions, there are fish that can endure every alternation of seasons, including floods and drought. Most fish will lose their lives during a dry season, except for a species of fish that has adapted. While the majority of fish get their necessary oxygen from the waters alone, these particular fish can breathe air. They have an ability to survive out of the water and can even travel on land between pools.

Even more impressive than this special species of fish, is a species of deep sea life that has the ability to survive in hydrothermal vents. The temperature of the waters surrounding those vents exceed the boiling point. Although hydrogen sulfide constantly shoots out of the vents, various wildlife surround it. These creatures manage to cope in a toxic, sunless habitat. For most life forms, this is an impossible environment.

There is also a species of parrots native to Nicaragua that nest in the Masaya volcano crater, which continually lets out sulfurous fumes. The parrots manage to nest in this kind of lethal environment that would kill other animals (and even humans) in a matter of a few minutes. Instead of harm or destruction coming upon these parrots, they manage to thrive and maintain their vitality in the most uncommon way.

The same God who created these amazing creatures with these extraordinary abilities has also created us. And He has endowed us with a nature to match the role that He has given us. You see, as Christian wives, we possess the power of God and the ability to adapt in every environment during every alternating season. Though the enemy preys on marriages and the family unit, we shall come out unharmed, unscathed, and without a scratch. Troubles may come that seem to exceed the boiling point, but you can survive the heat. You can maintain the life and strength of your marriage even in the midst of the most challenging situations. Whether in seasons of drought, storms, or floods, your marriage does not have to suffer irreversible damage or death itself. No matter how extreme the conditions seem to be, no matter how harsh or hostile the circumstances of life become, your marriage can survive. No matter how relentless the attacks on your marriage might be, it was meant to thrive. You may have already been through things that had the potential to destroy the average marriage, but yours endured in a most uncommon way.

It's time to become that wife of a new breed or species that is set apart from the norm. Learn to adapt. Adapt to a life as one, instead of that single life. Adapt yourself to him, thinking about and accommodating his needs rather than yours only. Adapt to every change on the path of your journey together. It's time to toughen up, ladies. When the going gets tough, the tough get going. No, not out the door! They get acclimated and they get adjusted. When it comes to the ups and downs of married life, if you can adapt yourself, your marriage can survive anything. And not just survive, but THRIVE!

How will you acclimate yourself to a change in your environment? How will you adapt when change comes—a change of luck, a change in jobs, a change in health, a change in the way you feel? A change in just about anything is possible, and you might find that things aren't the way they used to be when you first got married. What are you going to do about it? Adapt!

What changing conditions have I found difficult to adapt to in my marriage?

_____

_____

_____

_____

How can I maintain my vitality in spite of these difficulties?

_____

_____

_____

_____

Prayer

Thank You Lord for the power of Your Holy Spirit which dwells within me. You enable me to function successfully in any and every season of my life. It is in You that I live and move and have my being. I can do all things through Christ who strengthens me. He who is in me is greater than he that is in the world, therefore I have that *something extra* on the inside of me that puts me over and keeps me on top. Because I am adaptable, my marriage shall be made stronger. It will grow and flourish. My marriage shall come through every test with a testimony and every trial with this verdict: My marriage is one that survives and THRIVES!

PERSONAL REFLECTIONS

_____

_____

_____

_____

_____

_____

_____

_____

_____

_____

_____

_____

_____

_____

_____

_____

_____

_____

_____

I Follow My Husband's Guidance

*It was thus that Sarah obeyed Abraham [**following his guidance and acknowledging his headship over her by**] calling him lord (master, leader, authority). And you are now her true daughters if you do right and let nothing terrify you [not giving way to hysterical fears or letting anxieties unnerve you].*

1 Peter 3:6 (AMP)

As we began to see in the past few days, there is a great plan and purpose behind God's instruction for us to submit to our husbands. In placing ourselves under their God-given position of authority in our relationship and homes, we free them up to accomplish everything God has called them to without any hindrance. We place ourselves under one mission and assignment as a married couple. We adapt ourselves in a way that causes our marriage itself to thrive.

I,_____, take thee,_____, to be my wedded husband, to have and to hold from this day forward, for better or for worse, for richer or for poorer, in sickness and in health, to love, cherish, and to obey, till death do us part, according to God's holy ordinance.

Did you insert your name in the blanks when we looked at these commonly recited vows yesterday? These are the traditional wedding vows that once held a much more sacred meaning than they do today.

Few couples today opt to include the word *obey* in their vows. Is the word "obey" outdated?

> It was thus that Sarah obeyed Abraham [**following his guidance and acknowledging his headship over her by**] calling him lord (master, leader, authority). And you are now her true daughters if you do right and let nothing terrify you [not giving way to hysterical fears or letting anxieties unnerve you]. (1 Peter 3:6 AMP)

Let's take another look at our key verse for the day. I like the way the Amplified version spells out submission. We tend to define the word submit as "to obey." Here, the word obey is broken down a bit for us. Obey is defined as "in following his guidance and acknowledging his headship over." You see, subjection is an affectionate submission of the will. We willingly and voluntarily place ourselves under our husband's leadership and authority as the God-ordained head of our home. We don't do it out of dread. We don't do it out of fear or coercion, but out of a committing of ourselves to him. And we submit to our husbands out of obedience to the command of God.

> **Submit** – put yourself under, adapt yourselves, coming under the cover of your husband who is under the cover of Jesus Christ.

That cover is an umbrella of sorts that protects the wife from the fiery darts of Satan. That umbrella is the blood of Jesus.

The wife should willingly submit to her husband. The husband should be a loving, servant leader. But what if he is *not* the loving husband who is acting like the head of the house? What if he is not fulfilling his God-given responsibilities and role? Does that then give the wife the right to step in and take charge? Absolutely not. Verses 1 and 2 of 1 Peter 3, tell us that even when a husband is not a believer or not obeying the Lord, the wife is still to submit to him and treat him with the utmost respect. In this way, her right behavior will produce the right results; he may be won over to the Lord by her godly conduct. The wrong behavior, however, will never produce the kind of results that we hope for.

I have heard these words many times: "I have to take charge because he won't." Here are a couple of problems with that. First of all, when a wife steps into her husband's role, it is impossible for him to then walk in his God-given role because she is occupying that place.

God gives us grace to walk in *our* God given roles. He equips us to do what He has called *us* to do. When we take on someone else's role, one that doesn't belong to us and one that God did not give to us, there is no grace there. As long as a wife is walking in the husband's role, he cannot occupy it.

A wife must allow her husband to walk in his role even if he is not doing it perfectly. She must allow him to make mistakes. The more he practices it, the more he will grow in it. He must have the opportunity to grow.

A wife is very efficient in running her household. She is just wired that way. She takes charge of managing many things. She is the master of multi-tasking! She keeps things running smoothly like a well-oiled wheel. She is on top of things and she gets things done! She makes sure those children are doing what they are supposed to do, and she makes sure that they are productive too. She had better be careful though, careful to resist taking charge of her husband in the same way that she takes charge of her children. This is out of order. Her role as mother *does* include instructing and guiding the children, but nowhere in her role as wife is she to instruct and guide her husband. And her role absolutely does not include controlling her husband in any way. Being a good builder of your home requires knowing *who* is the head over the house.

> Wives, submit to your own husbands, as to the Lord. For the husband is head of the wife, as also Christ is head of the church; and He is the Savior of the body. (Ephesians 5:22-23 NKJV)

Headship means that God has called the man to *lead* his home and will therefore hold him responsible for what goes on in his home. The emphasis is on responsibility and accountability, not on authority and power to rule over.

This is pure freedom and relief to the wife who understands this. I used to interfere in every decision that I thought my husband was messing up. I felt responsible somehow to spare myself and the children from any consequences that might arise from going in what I thought might be the wrong direction for our family. Then the Lord spoke to me about this very thing. As my husband is the head of the home, *he* will be held accountable before God for any missteps, not me. That revelation was a great release to me. I no longer needed to push or pull. I was off the hook. I could relax and let him lead whether he did it perfectly or not.

My husband trusts me and values my opinion and insight. He will even ask me what I think about a matter. He does not, however, always follow my advice. It's okay! I am not always right. And even if I am sure that I am right, I allow him to have the final word on the matter. That is not always easy for a woman, but it is necessary.

I have learned that submission doesn't mean that I do not have a voice in my home. He hears me and considers what I have to say. If he goes in a direction decision-wise that is not what I thought was best, I continue to support him. I do it because I follow his guidance, and I follow his guidance because I acknowledge his headship. In this way, I honor him.

In the book of Titus, older women are instructed to "admonish the young women to love their husbands, to love their children, to be discreet, chaste, homemakers, good, **obedient to their own husbands**, that the word of God may not be blasphemed." (Titus 2:4-5 NKJV)

Here we see the word "obey" again (obedient). This is the word *hupotasso* in the original Greek language. It is the same word used in 1 Peter 3:1 (be submissive) and also in Ephesians 5:22 (submit). It literally translates "subordinate, put oneself under, submit self unto, yield to one's admonition or advice."

So you see, this word "obey" is not a degrading word that insinuates prisoner status, but it is a word that in reality brings about great freedom and protection. The wife is called to submit to her husband's leadership, respect, regard, and deeply care for him. This points to serving her husband, honoring him, and edifying or building him up. Her attitude, according to Ephesians 5:22 (as to the Lord) is to be one of highest esteem and regard. In *this* way she is contributing to bringing him into his full potential.

Can I follow my husband's guidance, or do I feel that I must guide him?

_____

_____

_____

_____

Can I relinquish control and allow him to lead unhindered, even if he doesn't lead perfectly?

_____

_____

_____

_____

Will I allow him to grow in his role as the leader and head of our home?

_____

_____

_____

Will I honor him in a way that will lead to his reaching his full potential?

_____

_____

_____

_____

Can I commit today to the instruction of the Lord to submit to my husband?

_____

_____

_____

_____

Prayer

Lord, today I acknowledge my husband's headship in our home. I am willing to submit to his leadership. I pray that he will grow into a strong leader. Guide him, Lord, as he guides our family. Cause his spiritual ears each day to hear You more clearly than the day before. Allow the inner compass of his spirit to follow Your direction for our lives together more closely than ever before. Cause him to become the righteous man whose footsteps are ordered by the Lord. Touch his life in a way that causes him to reach his full potential. Teach me when and how I can contribute to that. Thank You, Lord, for the freedom and protection that I have because of my husband's leadership.

THE PATH *to Becoming a* PROVERBS 31 WIFE

PERSONAL REFLECTIONS

_____

_____

_____

_____

_____

_____

_____

_____

_____

_____

_____

_____

_____

_____

_____

_____

_____

_____

_____

_____

Day 12

I Am One With My Husband

Wives, be subject (be submissive and adapt yourselves) to your own husbands as [a service] to the Lord. For the husband is head of the wife as Christ is the Head of the church, Himself the Savior of [His] body. **As the church is subject to Christ, so let wives also be subject in everything to their husbands.** *Husbands, love your wives, as Christ loved the church and gave Himself up for her, so that He might sanctify her, having cleansed her by the washing of water with the Word, that He might present the church to Himself in glorious splendor, without spot or wrinkle or any such things [that she might be holy and faultless]. Even so husbands should love their wives as [being in a sense] their own bodies. He who loves his own wife loves himself. For no man ever hated his own flesh, but nourishes and carefully protects and cherishes it, as Christ does the church, because we are members (parts) of His body. For this reason a man shall leave his father and his mother and* **shall be joined** *to his wife, and* **the two shall become one flesh.**

This mystery is very great, but I speak concerning [the relation of] Christ and the church.

However, let each man of you [without exception] love his wife as [being in a sense] his very own self; and **let the wife see that she respects and reverences her husband [that she notices him, regards him, honors him, prefers him, venerates, and esteems him; and that she defers to him, praises him, and loves and admires him exceedingly].**

Ephesians 5:22-33 (AMP)

We are beginning to see submission in a new light. Submission is protection and it is freedom! It brings about focused purpose. And it leads to unity, which releases the blessings of the Lord.

We submit to our husbands first and foremost because we have a desire to obey the Lord and please Him. At this point we can also clearly see that submission is birthed out of love and respect for our own husband. Submission also leads to unity.

From the beginning, a man leaves his father and mother and is joined to his wife. Likewise, the woman leaves her mother and father and is joined to her husband. Some translations use the words "cleaves" and "is yoked together."

To leave implies a priority change and this cleaving is better described as "gluing or so firmly adhering to one another that nothing and no one can separate them." They are no longer separate. They do not continue to have separate interests but act as one. To cleave actually means "to cling to, to pursue hard after, and to follow closely." It means "to be united closely in interest and affection; to adhere with strong attachment, to be stitched together, to keep close, to stick with or to stay with."

To be joined together is better translated "to be yoked together." It is the word or term *suzeugnumi* in the Greek and it is a picture of the oxen being yoked together in the plow where each must pull equally in order to bring it forward. Being joined together is being so closely tied and united that a husband and wife are pulling equally together in all the concerns of life. They are moving together as one. Their hearts are set on the same mission.

A husband and wife are no longer focused on their own wants, desires, and needs, but now have a brand new focus. That focus must become one. Two people continuing to pursue their own separate, self-centered, or self-seeking desires will quickly be in conflict. The Proverb 31 wife, whom we have been looking at as our model, is clearly *not* self-seeking. Love, as described in 1 Corinthians 13, is *not* self-seeking. Love doesn't desire to get its own way.

Two people remaining separate in the marriage relationship will be in a constant state of conflict. Conflict breeds division, not unity. And we know that a house divided against itself cannot stand...

Jack Hayford says this about the vital unity between a husband and wife: "From the beginning God's heart to build a dwelling place for Himself in the Earth is seen in His creation of man and woman— together, the foundation of the house of the Lord. Through the two of them together, He intended to live and reveal Himself in the world. Through them, God intended to manifest His character and authority (image), express His dominion over the [e]arth, display His indisputable power over the works of darkness, and subdue His archenemy, Satan. The first man and woman were a microcosm of the church, signaling that God's glory would forever be seen in the [e]arth through the combined expression of male and female. Now, as then, God's blessing—His promise of success—is upon our unity."

This oneness, this unity in our marriages, is so important. Hayford states that God's *promise of success* is upon our unity. I believe that! I am also reminded of Psalm 133:1-3, which says, "Behold, how good and how pleasant it is for brethren to dwell together in unity! It is like the precious oil upon the head, running down on the beard, the beard of Aaron, running down on the edge of his garments. It is like the dew of Hermon, descending upon the mountains of Zion; for there the Lord commanded the blessing – life forevermore." (NKJV)

There, in the place of unity, the Lord *commands* the blessing. Not only does He command blessings and promises of success upon the marriage as you both become one, but He desires to reveal Himself to the world through the relationship of a husband and wife. If this is the case (and it is), then our greatest mission as a married couple is to reflect Jesus Christ. It is to put Christ on display. There is a much bigger picture here. Marriage is a small thing that is part of a bigger picture. Therefore, we don't have time to fuss and fight. We don't have time to demand our own way. We must come to a realization that our Christian marriages are a picture, a portrait, of Christ and the Church, His deep and sacrificial love for His people. Time is short. If we are to be that kind of image bearer, it is time to get it together and present an accurate picture to the world. It is time to once and for all truly become one with our spouse.

> Therefore shall a man leave his father and his mother,
> and shall cleave unto his wife: and they shall be one flesh.
> (Genesis 2:24 KJV)

Are we operating as one, or is there division in the house?

_____

_____

_____

_____

Is there a greater purpose for my marriage?

_____

_____

_____

_____

Do we have a common goal or mission that cements us together as one?

_____

_____

_____

What is our calling as a couple? What important assignment does God have for us together as one?

_____

_____

_____

Is Christ revealed to the world through our union?

_____

_____

_____

What must I do to become one with my husband?

_____

_____

_____

Prayer

Lord, truly join and yoke my husband and I together as one. Stitch us together. Bond us in a way that goes beyond what we have yet experienced. Unite us together both in interest and affection. Mature our love for one another that we might put Christ on display through our marriage relationship. Accomplish Your purposes in our lives, not only as two individuals, but most importantly as one. Command Your blessing upon our unity. Thank You that Your promises are "yes" and "amen" toward us in Christ Jesus.

PERSONAL REFLECTIONS

_____

_____

_____

_____

_____

_____

_____

_____

_____

_____

_____

_____

_____

_____

_____

_____

_____

My Love Story is But a Reflection of the Greatest Love Story Ever Told

For this reason a man shall leave his father and mother and be joined to his wife, and the two shall become one flesh.

Ephesians 5:31 (NKJV)

The Proverbs 31 wife is a great model to learn from and follow, but we have another model, and that model is Christ. In fact, when it comes specifically to the marriage relationship, according to Ephesians 5, that model is Christ's relationship to His church.

Ephesians 5:22-33 talks about how the husband and wife are to relate to one another in sacrificial love, honor, and respect. The husband and wife are to do this in the way modeled by Christ in His love for His church. All throughout scripture we can find this language of love which refers to Christ as the Bridegroom and His church as His bride. Most Bible scholars agree that from the very beginning, marriage was designed by God to symbolize the relationship of Christ to the church.

Wait a minute—that's pretty deep. A Christian marriage is supposed to symbolize the relationship of Christ to the church? If that is the case, my husband and I have a responsibility to reflect that correctly.

In verse 25, husbands are instructed to love their wives *as Christ loved the church and gave Himself up for her, redeeming and sanctifying her.* We know this love story well, don't we? It is the greatest love story ever told! Our sin separated us from God, but while we were yet sinners, Christ loved us and died for us. When we deserved death and Hell, He demonstrated His love for us. Christ left his Father's home in Heaven and came to earth to live a sinless life so that He might redeem us. Jesus, who was without sin, paid the penalty of sin for us that we might be reconciled to God. He did something for us that we could not have done for ourselves. By laying down His life, He provided a way for us to be forgiven and one day spend eternity in Heaven with Him. Through His great sacrifice, we can be delivered and healed. Because of His death and resurrection, we can have full, meaningful, abundant life right now. All these provisions were made out of His passion and great love for us. All of these benefits we possess came through Christ's own suffering, pain, rejection, and self-sacrifice. That was His way of love, and what a beautiful love story it is.

Because of His great love, Christ laid down his life for us and verse 31 of Ephesians 5 says, for this reason, a man shall leave his father and mother and be joined together to his wife. For *what* reason...? That this mystery of Christ's love for His church might be on display through our marriages.

If, indeed, marriage was designed by God from the very beginning to model or reflect Christ's love for His church, how are we doing? Are our marriages showing the world an accurate picture?

It is God's desire to form an intimate union with His people, a connection with Himself. He desires to have such an intimate communion with His people that they would become one with Him. This is the way of love, and our marriage relationships are to be a portrait of this great love!

If our marriages can be a testimony, a witness, and an image of something greater—Christ's love for His people—what kind of image bearers have we been?

If the Bridegroom's love for His bride is on display through our own marriages, does my marriage really resemble Christ's story of love?

Can the witness of our love for one for another in our marriages really have an impact on a lost and dying world around us? If so, what kind of impact is it making now? Am I displaying the gospel message in my marriage?

Is my marriage representing the attitude and conduct of Christ, and does it point to something bigger—the reality of Jesus Christ's relationship to His church? Is this marriage an earthly symbol of a heavenly reality?

No wonder the enemy of our souls seeks to destroy the sanctity of marriage. No wonder he works so hard to destroy the family. His goal is to distort and pervert the symbol and type of Christ's love for His people! Marriage, therefore, must be protected.

What is my part as a wife? How do I contribute to this visible picture for all to see the love between Christ and His bride, the church? A wife represents the church in the way she relates to her husband. She fulfills a unique role.

The church, in its relationship to Christ, is to honor Him, respect, revere, trust, submit to Him in all things, and respond to Him in love. The bride of Christ is to be a faithful bride. She has her life wrapped up in His, serving Him and loving Him. Am I representing this model accurately as a wife?

> He said, "This is the blood of the covenant, which God has commanded you to keep." In the same way, he sprinkled with the blood both the tabernacle and everything used in its ceremonies. In fact, the law requires that nearly everything be cleansed with blood, and without the shedding of blood there is no forgiveness. It was necessary, then, for **the copies of the heavenly things** to be purified with these sacrifices, but the heavenly things themselves with better sacrifices than these. For

Christ did not enter a sanctuary made with human hands that
was only a copy of the true one; he entered heaven itself, now
to appear for us in God's presence. (Hebrews 9:20-24 NIV)

God many times uses things on earth to symbolize and point to spiritual
realities—heavenly things, holy things. They are symbols, types, or
copies. Truth for today: My marriage is but a copy of something bigger
and better.

In what ways do I need to come into alignment that I might become a
true testimony for Christ in and through my marriage?

_____

_____

_____

_____

How can my marriage be a symbol of the spiritual reality of God's
holy love?

_____

_____

_____

_____

Prayer

Lord, this lends new meaning to my responsibility before You, to walk
in love toward my husband. I must cleave and be yoked together with
him, instead of fighting and pulling against him. I must attach myself to
him in a way that Your love would be on display through our marriage.
Show me the way of love that I may walk in it. Help me to be the best
witness and representation that I can be so that Your glory might be
revealed to the world.

PERSONAL REFLECTIONS

_____

_____

_____

_____

_____

_____

_____

_____

_____

_____

_____

_____

_____

_____

_____

_____

_____

_____

_____

I Follow Christ's Example in the Way That I Love

See what great love the Father has lavished on us, that we should be called children of God! And that is what we are! The reason the world does not know us is that it did not know him.

1 John 3:1 (NIV)

The KJV uses the word "behold." "Behold, look, or see what manner of love the Father hath bestowed upon us..." Today we need to take a fresh look at just what kind of love He extends to us that we might imitate that kind of love in our marriages. The world might just get a glimpse of His love and believe! Are you ready to offer the hope of God's love to the world through the testimony of your marriage?

God has a GREAT love for you and for me, and the Bible tells us that He lavishes it upon us. To lavish means "to give unsparingly." It is a love that is given in an unrestrained way. To lavish means "to shower, pour, or heap." It is excessive, immoderate, bountiful, and profuse! It is rich and elaborate. Lavish means "to bestow something in generous or extravagant quantities." God's love is more than enough!

To lavish means to be overgenerous. That is very interesting because Proverbs 31:11 tells us that the Proverb 31 wife is "never spiteful, **she treats him generously all her life long.**" (Proverbs 31:11 MSG)

I believe that the Proverbs 31 wife was generous in her love toward her husband. I believe that she was following Christ's example in the way that she loved her husband and that we can follow His example too.

> "See what [an incredible] quality of love the Father has given (shown, bestowed on) us…" (1 John 3:1 AMP)

> "What marvelous love the Father has extended to us!" (1 John 3:1 MSG)

His love is of an incredible quality and quantity! It is a marvelous love. It is a great love, the kind of love that does not hold back but is given unsparingly.

Paul prayed that the Ephesians would truly grasp just "how wide, and long, and high, and deep is the love of God." (Ephesians 3:18 NIV). It is a love that goes beyond ordinary parameters. The enemy continuously attacks us in the area of the way that we love so that the world will never get a glimpse of His great love. Those of us who have experienced His love must also demonstrate it.

Romans 5:8 tells us that while we were yet sinners, while we were yet God's enemies, He loved us and gave Himself for us. Before we demonstrated any kind of love toward Him, He demonstrated His love toward us. When we were unlovable, He loved us. When we didn't deserve His love, He didn't hold His love back from us. Instead, He lavished it upon us. When we didn't reciprocate that love, He loved us anyway. His feelings and emotions didn't hold Him on that cross. Neither should our feelings and emotions alone dictate to us how we will love our husbands. We must love them with the love of Christ, the kind of love that is unrelenting, the kind of love that just doesn't give up.

Romans 8:38-40 tells us more about this great love of Christ: "…neither death, nor life, nor angels, nor principalities, nor things present and threatening, nor things to come, nor powers, nor height nor depth, nor any other created thing, will be able to separate us from the [unlimited] love of God, which is in Christ Jesus our Lord." (AMP)

Nothing, nothing, nothing, can separate us from the love of God, "not trouble, not hard times, not hatred, not hunger, not loneliness, not bullying threats, not backstabbing, not even the worst sins listed in Scripture." "Nothing living or dead, angelic or demonic" nothing "today or tomorrow," nothing "high or low," nothing "thinkable or unthinkable," nothing "absolutely nothing can get between us and God's love because the way that Jesus our Master has embraced us." (Romans 8:38-39 MSG)

Now that is an incredible love! Nothing can separate us from it, not even past sins and failure. Nothing you have done or not done. His love is not earned or even deserved. It is a free gift. He loves us with a high quality, extravagant, perfect, unconditional, unfailing love. What might happen if today I made a commitment to love my husband in this same manner? What might happen if I followed Christ's example in the way that I love my husband?

Do you need to make a brand new commitment today to follow Christ's example in the way that you love your spouse?

_____

_____

_____

_____

Samuele Bacchiocchi, author of *The Marriage Covenant*, says that many times that kind of commitment looks a lot like the way of the cross in this way: "growth in our marital commitment often takes place through deaths and resurrections. There are times in our marital relationship when communication becomes very difficult, if not impossible. Hurt, hostility, and resentment seem to prevail. Yet, as we learn by God's grace to put to death and to bury all such ill-feelings, out of that dying, new life comes in our relationship."

In what ways do I need to take up my cross today that I might experience new life in my marriage relationship?

_____

_____

_____

_____

Is there anything keeping me from lavishing my love upon my husband? If so, am I willing to put that thing to death today?

_____

_____

_____

_____

Prayer

Lord, I have made a decision today to love my husband with a love of high quality and quantity. And I am not going to wait until he loves me like this first. I am pondering what might happen if I poured out my love upon him in this way. What barriers might be broken down? Lord, teach me to love my husband. Help me to follow Your example in the way that I love him. Breathe new life into our marriage relationship today. In Jesus' name I pray.

PERSONAL REFLECTIONS

My Marriage Is Holy

*Then the rib which the Lord God had taken from man, He
made into a woman, and He brought her to the man.*

*And Adam said: "This is now bone of my bones
And flesh of my flesh; she shall be called Woman,
Because she was taken out of Man."*

*Therefore a man shall leave his father and mother and be
joined to his wife, and they shall become one flesh.*

Genesis 2:22-24 (NKJV)

"Dearly beloved, we are gathered together here in the sight of God,
and in the face of this company, to join together this man and this
woman in *holy matrimony…*"

What makes a marriage holy? Is my marriage holy?

> **Holy** – associated with divine power, sacred, consecrated,
> set apart for God to be as it were exclusively His, pure and
> clean, regarded with special respect or reverence, having
> a highly moral or spiritual purpose, exalted or worthy of
> complete devotion.

Think back to the day that you said, "I do." Did you marry your
husband because you fell in love and wanted to spend the rest of your
life with him? Did everything in your heart say, "This is the one for
me!" Did you dream of raising a family together and living happily
ever after? Probably so. You may have also regarded the institution

of marriage as sacred. Maybe you have worked really hard to keep it pure and clean. It is possible that, from the very beginning, you and your spouse set your marriage apart for God, dedicated it to Him, and vowed to always keep Him at the center of it. Some of us did. Some of us, however, were never really aware that there was any purpose for marriage other than our own. Up until now, it is possible that you have never considered God's point of view. If God does have a highly moral or spiritual purpose for your marriage, wouldn't it be worthy of your complete devotion?

Marriage, or holy matrimony as we are calling it today, was instituted by God Himself. First of all, it is referred to as "holy matrimony" because it comes from Him. It was His idea from the beginning to be a holy and lasting covenant. Not only did He institute this covenant, but He demonstrated to us how to keep it.

What is a covenant? The word "covenant" is a biblical word. It is of Latin origin (*con venine*) and means "a coming together." It is when two or more parties come together to make a lasting and binding agreement with promises, stipulations, privileges, and responsibilities. The Old Testament uses the word covenant 280 times (the Hebrew word is *berit*) and is most accurately translated as "promise or pledge." The New Testament uses the word covenant thirty-three times (the Greek word is *diatheke*) and it most frequently means "a bond or a pact."

On your wedding day, you made a covenant with your husband in the presence of God. In many ways, your wedding ceremony itself resembled the practices of ancient covenant making.

Ancient covenants were always very solemn and serious agreements. First, everyone involved considered the agreement. The terms and conditions were outlined. They counted the cost of entering into the covenant and then they responded. Almost every covenant called upon one or more witnesses. Sacrifices were almost always included. Some sort of token was exchanged as a symbol of the two individuals' desire to no longer live independently. Common tokens were things like robes, belts, or weapons. If robes were exchanged, it symbolized the putting on of each other and becoming one. It also symbolized the taking on of a new position, a new character, and a new authority. Belts, which were a part of the armor, symbolized the giving of one's strengths and also the taking on of one's weaknesses. When weapons were exchanged as a token, it symbolized the commitment of defeating each other's enemies. The token itself was to be a seal which became the mark of the covenant, reminding both parties of the pact that bound them together as one.

Other customs of ancient covenant making included what they referred to as "the walk unto death." The two parties, or a representative from each party, would walk around the pieces of a sacrificed animal in a figure eight and then face each other. In this way, they were pledging to fulfill their obligations to keep the covenant. It was a vow unto death in order to fulfill their side of the pact. While the two parties stood in the middle of the sacrifice, each would pronounce aloud the terms of the covenant. Often a promise or blessing would be involved. It was also common to exchange names, implying an exchange of personality, character, reputation, and authority. A covenant meal was shared in celebration. The meal always included bread and wine, which represented the body and the blood of the covenant partners. As they celebrated the meal, they made their concluding declaration that they would live as one. And from that day forward, others viewed them as one.

In ancient times, covenants were made between individuals, tribes, and nations. Commonly, the covenant's purpose was for protection, strength, or prosperity. These covenants were taken very seriously. There was a sacredness about the vows they took, and they were meant to be kept and not broken.

In the word of God, we read about people making covenants with other people and most importantly, God Himself making covenants with His people. God made a covenant with Noah, Abraham, Moses, and David. And He made a covenant with His people, Israel, on Mount Sinai, one that the prophets speak of as a marriage covenant.

God is a covenant-making, covenant-keeping God. He has set a pattern for us to follow that is found within the covenant that He has made with His people. Before we take a look at that covenant, let's consider our own vows and commitments and just what they mean to us today.

Before I gave myself to my husband in holy matrimony, did I count the cost and was I willing to pay it?

_____

_____

_____

_____

Has there ever been a time that I have consecrated my marriage to God, setting it apart for Him?

_____

_____

_____

Have I maintained a pure and clean heart in my marriage?

_____

_____

_____

_____

Have I kept the terms and conditions of my marriage covenant? Do I intend to fulfill my every promise, pledge, and vow?

_____

_____

_____

_____

My husband and I exchanged wedding rings on our wedding day as the token or symbol of the marriage covenant we made that day. What does my wedding ring symbolize and represent to me?

_____

_____

_____

_____

Do I view my marriage covenant as permanent and broken only by death? In my heart, is it settled that this marriage is for life, or have I been leaving my options open?

_____

_____

_____

_____

How seriously have I taken my marriage covenant? Do I regard it with respect and reverence? Do I need to renew this covenant in my own heart today?

_____

_____

_____

_____

Prayer

Lord, today I dedicate my marriage to you in a fresh new way. I consecrate it and set it apart for Your purposes. In my heart, I renew my vows and promises. I will honor my commitment to my husband before the Lord as long as I live. I will not entertain thoughts of any other options. I am not looking for a way out. I regard my marriage as a sacred union and a holy matrimony. Because marriage is from You, Lord, it is worthy of my complete devotion. And my complete devotion is what I am willing to give.

PERSONAL REFLECTIONS

_____

_____

_____

_____

_____

_____

_____

_____

Day 16

I Am A Covenant Keeper

*The Lord did not set his affection on you and choose you because you were more numerous than other peoples, for you were the fewest of all peoples. But it was because the Lord loved you and kept the oath he swore to your ancestors that he brought you out with a mighty hand and redeemed you from the land of slavery, from the power of Pharaoh King of Egypt. **Know therefore that the Lord your God is God; he is the faithful God, keeping his covenant of love to a thousand generations of those who love him and keep his commandments.***

Deuteronomy 7:7-9 (NIV)

God is a covenant making God. He has set a pattern for us to follow and He has demonstrated to us how to be a covenant keeper.

God made a covenant with His people and it was a covenant of love. The people didn't necessarily deserve His love though. They didn't always reciprocate it either. God, however, remained faithful to His covenant of love.

It all began on Mount Sinai. During the exodus from Egypt, God entered into a sacred relationship with His people known as a covenant (Exodus 20). The relationship established that day was more than the giving of the law or 10 Commandments. A relational bond was being established. As the prophets retell the events of Mount Sinai, they describe them in terms of a young bride being wooed by her divine bridegroom to enter into a marriage with Him (Hosea 2:14-15, Jeremiah 2:1-2, Ezekiel 16).

"When I passed by you again and looked upon you, indeed
your time was the time of love; so I spread My wing over you
and covered your nakedness. Yes, I swore an oath to you and
entered into a covenant with you, and you became Mine," says
the Lord GOD. (Ezekiel 16:8 NKJV)

The people, however, were unfaithful and abandoned their covenant,
turning to idols. Generation after generation, they were an unfaithful
people, but God's love for His people was unrelenting. He continued to
reveal His love to them through the prophets.

God told the prophet Hosea to marry a prostitute named Gomer and
raise a family with her. In doing so, Hosea was demonstrating God's
covenant of love. When Gomer went after other lovers, God told
Hosea to take her back and love her again. In doing so, He was acting
out God's unrelenting love, the kind of love that just doesn't stop. God
was revealing Himself as a forgiving, compassionate, and loving spouse.

"And it shall be, in that day," says the Lord, "that you will
call Me 'My Husband,' and no longer call Me 'My Master.' I
will betroth you to Me forever; Yes, I will betroth you to Me
in righteousness and justice, in lovingkindness and mercy; I
will betroth you to Me in faithfulness, and you shall know the
Lord…" (Hosea 2:16,19-20 NKJV)

The prophet Jeremiah reminded the people of their covenant
relationship with God. Even though they had broken the covenant,
God would remain faithful. It was a love that just would not let go. He
promised to one day forgive His bride and establish a new covenant
with her. This was their hope, that God Himself would restore
the broken relationship, renew the covenant, and do the work of
transforming their hearts.

"Behold, the days are coming," says the LORD, "when I will
make a new covenant with the house of Israel and with the

house of Judah— not according to the covenant that I made with their fathers in the day that I took them by the hand to lead them out of the land of Egypt, My covenant which they broke, though I was a husband to them," says the LORD. "But this is the covenant that I will make with the house of Israel after those days," says the LORD: "I will put My law in their minds, and write it on their hearts; and I will be their God, and they shall be My people." (Jeremiah 31:31-33 NKJV)

Through the prophet Ezekiel, God revealed Himself as a Husband wooing and winning back an unfaithful wife and reestablishing a lasting covenant with His bride.

"Nevertheless I will remember My covenant with you in the days of your youth, and I will establish an everlasting covenant with you....And I will establish My covenant with you. Then you shall know that I am the Lord, that you may remember and be ashamed, and never open your mouth anymore because of your shame, when I provide you an atonement for all you have done," says the Lord GOD." (Ezekiel 16:60, 62-63 NKJV)

In the Old Testament, we can see God's plan to wed Himself to humankind in an everlasting marriage covenant, a covenant where love prevails! This beautiful love story continues to unfold and be fulfilled in the New Testament when Christ gave Himself for us as He was crucified, expressing his spousal love for us. We see the nature of His love in His complete devotion to His bride. It is Christ's total commitment in the giving of Himself in which the Christian marriage is to be founded upon.

In the New Testament, when Jesus was addressing questions about marriage, His response revealed that it is God Himself who actually joins a couple in marriage (Mark 10:5-9). He is the author *and* the witness (Malachi 2:13-14) of this divinely ordained union, making the marriage covenant all the more binding.

Paul followed the teaching of Jesus in Romans 7:1-3, stating that the marriage covenant is to be a lifelong covenant. In Ephesians chapter 5, Paul uses the marriage union to illustrate the covenant relationship between Christ and His bride, the church.

In the Old Testament, the relationship between God and Israel is portrayed as a marriage covenant. In the New Testament, the marriage union represents Christ's covenant of sacrificial love and oneness with the church. The picture of the marriage relationship is found throughout the Bible from beginning to end.

God has given us a model and a pattern to follow when it comes to loving our spouse and keeping our marriage vows. The most amazing thing is that He has given us imperfect, emotional, and often inconsistent women the absolute power and ability to do just that. He has purposed that the Christian marriage be a reflection of His divine love. Therefore, a Christian marriage is sacred. It is, indeed, a holy matrimony. My marriage is a divinely ordained union. I have made a covenant of love with my husband. And I am determined to be a covenant keeper.

In what ways can I follow the model that Christ has given me?

_____

_____

_____

_____

There will be times when I feel that my husband doesn't necessarily deserve my demonstration of love. Will I love him anyway?

_____

_____

_____

There will be times when my expression of love will not be reciprocated in the way that I had hoped or expected that it would be. Will I love him anyway? Will I continue in a steadfast, unrelenting kind of love?

_____

_____

_____

_____

Has my marriage covenant suffered brokenness in any way? Will I trust God to do the work of restoring the broken relationship?

_____

_____

_____

_____

Am I willing to be a forgiving, compassionate, and loving spouse?

_____

_____

_____

_____

Prayer

Lord, marriage was Your idea from the very beginning. You instituted the covenant of marriage. I understand the sacredness of my marriage union better today than ever before. Thank You for Your covenant of love that You have established with Your people. I am in a covenant relationship with You, Lord. I find great peace, assurance, and rest in knowing that You are faithful to keep Your promises to me. Even when

I have been unfaithful to You, You have always remained faithful to me. To say that I am grateful for Your faithfulness does not come close to expressing to You what that means to me. It is not easy to love the way that You love, Lord, but You have given me the power to do just that. I realize that there will be days when I will feel like my husband doesn't necessarily deserve my love or my faithfulness. Nevertheless, I will love him and continue to be faithful. I will follow You in loving him in an unconditional, unrelenting way. I will love him with a love that just doesn't stop. I will be a forgiving, compassionate, and loving spouse. Restore what's been broken, Lord. Help me to love him with a total commitment in the giving of myself. Reestablish a strong and lasting covenant within my marriage. I honor my wedding vows. I will keep my every promise. Like Christ, I will be a covenant keeper.

PERSONAL REFLECTIONS

_____

_____

_____

_____

_____

_____

_____

_____

_____

_____

Day 17

I Keep My Heart Clear

"Since you have purified your souls in obeying the truth through the Spirit in sincere love of the brethren, love one another fervently with a pure heart."
1 Peter 1:22 (NKJV)

It is not always easy to love. Let's face it, some people are just hard to love. And that husband that in the beginning swept you off your feet? Sometimes he is hard to love too. If you have been married for any length of time, you have discovered that love is not necessarily a feeling or an emotion. It is a choice. It is a decision. It is a commitment. And if you are going to keep your vow to love and honor that man all the days of your life, there are some truths from the word of God that you are going to need to follow. First Peter gives us some very important instructions on how to love, and these principles certainly apply to loving our husbands.

Your soul includes your mind, your will, and your emotions. Where does the enemy attack us? You guessed it—in our minds and in our emotions, which directly influence our will and, of course, our actions.

How do we purify our souls? The word purify means "to make clean or to make clear." The word soul also translates "your life and your vitality." There are things that you will encounter that have the potential to suck the very life and vitality right out of you and right out of your marriage. We must make clear our minds, emotions, and will.

Hurt and offense will come. We will be rubbed the wrong way. There will be conflict. We cannot, however, allow these things to stick to our hearts. We must clear them away. We must clear them away quickly. We must clear them away today, so that we can continue loving tomorrow. Is your heart clear towards your husband today?

1 Peter 1:22 says, "Since you have purified your souls **in obeying the truth through the Spirit...**"

How do you make clear your soul or your heart? You begin by obeying the truth. First we must obey the Lord, who is the Truth. We must obey His word, His commandments, and His instructions. Secondly, we must remember that the enemy attacks our minds and emotions with lies. He is a liar. The Bible says that he is the father of lies, and that there is no truth in him. The enemy will interject a lie into your mind which affects you in your emotions and influences your will. You must be able to recognize the truth from a lie. The Spirit of God will give you discernment! We must refuse to react to the lies of the enemy concerning all things and especially concerning our spouses. The enemy feeds you lies like, "My husband doesn't love me. He doesn't appreciate me. He doesn't respect me..." and on and on until you are convinced that you are unhappy in your marriage. Woman of God, you don't have time to listen or respond to those kind of lies sent to you from the pit of Hell. Reject them. Keep your mind, will, and emotions clear!

Let's go a little further. "Since you have purified your souls in obeying the truth through the Spirit **in sincere love** of the brethren, love fervently with a pure heart."

Obey the truth in what area? The enemy, as I have said before, attacks the area of the way we love. Our love is to be sincere, meaning without hypocrisy. The verse goes on to say, "love one another fervently with a pure heart."

To love fervently is "to be eager to love, to be determined to love, to love on purpose, intently or intentionally." It also means "to love continually or without ceasing."

In 1 Peter 2:17, we are urged to honor, value, and respect one another. Can we love our husbands with a sincere and fervent love while honoring, respecting, and valuing them? Absolutely! We love like this by keeping our hearts clear. And keeping our hearts clear includes walking in forgiveness. When it comes to forgiveness, like Christ, we must have an all or nothing attitude and commitment.

> Therefore as the elect of God, holy and beloved, put on tender mercies, kindness, humility, meekness, longsuffering; bearing with one another, and forgiving one another, if anyone has a complaint against another; even as Christ forgave you, so you also just do. (Colossians 3:12-13 NKJV)

The word "forgiving" here is the word *charizomai* and it means "to do a favor, show kindness unconditionally, give freely, and grant forgiveness." The word is from the same root as *charis*, meaning "grace."

> Forgiveness is made possible through Christ, who forgave us. It is an act in which one person releases another from an offense, refusing to enact the penalty due him or her, refusing to sustain consideration of the cause of the offense, and refusing to allow that offense to affect the relationship. Such forgiveness releases one from a sense of unresolved guilt, restores a clear conscience, and restores relationship. To forgive is not to condone the sin as acceptable, to say it made no difference, or to license repetition of it. Rather, forgiveness is a choice—a decision made to no longer hold an offense against another person or group. – Raleigh B. Washington

The truth is, we look most like Christ when we forgive.

So, **chosen by God for this new life of love,** dress in the wardrobe God picked out for you: compassion, kindness, humility, quiet strength, discipline. Be even-tempered, content with second place, quick to forgive an offense. Forgive as quickly and completely as the Master forgave you. And regardless of what else you put on, wear love. It's your basic, all-purpose garment. **Never be without it.** (Colossians 3:12-14 MSG)

You have been *chosen* by God for this new life of love! God never chooses or calls anyone to do something that He hasn't also equipped and empowered them to do. Woman of God, you got this!

What lies have I believed about my husband and about my marriage?

_____

_____

_____

_____

What must I do today to make my heart clear toward my husband?

_____

_____

_____

_____

What must I do to keep my heart clear toward my husband every day?

_____

_____

_____

_____

Prayer

Lord, give me the discernment to know the difference between the truth and a lie concerning my relationship with my husband. Ignite new life and vitality in my marriage, I pray. My desire is to love my husband fervently with a pure heart. I am eager to love him. I will love him continually. I will walk in forgiveness. I will keep my heart clear. My heart is free to love and honor my husband all the days of my life.

PERSONAL REFLECTIONS

_____

_____

_____

_____

_____

_____

_____

_____

_____

_____

_____

_____

_____

_____

_____

_____

_____

_____

_____

_____

_____

_____

_____

_____

_____

_____

_____

_____

_____

_____

_____

_____

_____

_____

_____

Day 18

I Handle Conflict Correctly

Finally, all of you, be of one mind, having compassion for one another, love as brothers, be tenderhearted, be courteous, not returning evil for evil or reviling for reviling, **but on the contrary, blessing. Knowing that you were called to this,** *that you might inherit a blessing.*

1 Peter 3:8-9 (NKJV)

I am instructed by the Lord to love in a sincere and fervent way, respecting and honoring my husband while I keep my heart clear. That sounds wonderful, but what practical steps do I take to achieve that, especially in times when I am not being treated the same? The answer to that question is found in 1 Peter 3:8-9, specifically in verse nine.

Once again we are exhorted to be of one mind, like-minded and in unity. We are also instructed to have a heart of compassion for one another. Other versions of this scripture use words like "kind" and "humble." It does take a humble spirit to exercise the next part of the instructions: "...not returning evil for evil, reviling for reviling" (intended harm, insult, sarcasm...) with the same! Instead, we are told to do the *opposite* and do it knowing that we were "called to this." Called to what? **We were called to bless!**

In all of our roles, including helpmate, virtuous wife, home builder, encourager, covenant keeper...we are also called to be women who bless.

This is not only a practical step to having a clear heart that is free to love the way Christ loves, but it is also a very effective weapon. God has given us a weapon to demolish the enemy of our souls in this area of our lives. It is a weapon that will set you free if you will take hold of it.

When something ugly comes at you, bless. When you are insulted, bless.

When injury to your emotions comes, bless! Do what seems contrary. Do the opposite! It disarms the enemy. His purpose for harm is thwarted. His plan to subtract something from you and your marriage is canceled!

It is wrong thinking when you say to yourself, "I am going to treat my husband exactly the way he is treating me! If he is being very sweet to me, then I will be sweet to him. If he is being rude and hateful, then I will give it back to him!" I know that we are all human, but the truth is that this kind of response is always counterproductive anyway. We must do the opposite and bless!

Just exactly what does it mean to bless? The word "blessing" here is the Greek word *eulogeō*. *Eulogeō* translates "to invoke a benediction upon or to speak well of (religiously)." This word is from a compound of *eu*, meaning "good," and *logos*, meaning "something said or something spoken."

In the Old Testament and in the Jewish culture, the blessing was extremely important. There was something very powerful about imparting a blessing, so powerful that you and I will do well if we take notice and apply these principles in our marriages and homes.

Fathers would bless their children. They would lay hands upon their children and pronounce and speak a blessing over them, speaking their wishes and desires over them as well as God's word. Think about that—a parent, out of a parent's love, only desires the very best for their child. There is no doubt that the parent saw their child's issues, weaknesses, and struggles. Those things would be evident to them. Therefore, the blessing would sometimes include cursing the negative thing. The blessing would also include speaking success over every area of struggle or failure.

An example of this kind of spoken blessing over a struggling adult child might be, "I curse lack and struggle in your life, in Jesus' name. I speak a more than enough blessing over you. I bless you to walk in prosperity. You will succeed in all that you do. May all things abound to you!" You get the idea...

The parent also recognized the child's strengths, gifts, calling, and potential. The parent would bless the coming forth of those things and speak fruitfulness over them. Parents imparted life and success to their children through the spoken blessing. The building of godly character was one of the benefits and byproducts of the children receiving the blessing.

The spoken blessing is still practiced in many Jewish families and homes today. There is still something very powerful about imparting a blessing. My husband and I have started speaking a blessing over one another on a regular basis. I cannot even begin to tell you what kind of things have been released as a result. It has also created a stronger bond between us in a way that I have not yet found words to express. I want to challenge you as wives to begin speaking blessings over your husband, regularly and very intentionally.

When God created Adam and Eve, He spoke a blessing over them (Genesis 1:28, 5:2). Abraham, Isaac, and Jacob spoke blessings over their children (Genesis 27:21-29, 33-38). God commanded Moses to have Aaron and his sons speak blessings over the people:

> The LORD bless you and keep you; the LORD make His face to shine upon you, and be gracious to you; the LORD lift up His countenance upon you, and give you peace.
> (Numbers 6:24-26 NKJV)

Through this priestly blessing, Moses and Aaron invoked God's name. God was present in the blessing and imparted life to the people. This priestly blessing was released at the end of worship before dismissing the people. They were to carry the benefits of the blessing with them to their homes and their families. The effects of these blessings were experienced in every area of their lives. The priestly blessing given in Numbers 6:24-26 demonstrated the importance of the entire family in this time of blessing.

In the New Testament, we find Jesus taking the children in His arms, putting His hands upon them, and blessing them (Mark 10:16). One of the last things we find Jesus doing before He ascends to Heaven is imparting a blessing to His disciples. He led them out as far as Bethany, and He lifted up His hands and He blessed them (Luke 24:50-51).

The beatitudes in Matthew chapter 5 are a series of blessings. It is important to understand that the disciples had many flaws when Jesus called them "the salt of the earth" and the "light of the world." At that time, they were neither of those things, yet Jesus called them just that. Jesus saw beyond their present and temporary flaws and failures. He saw their potential. He saw the possibilities. He spoke a blessing over them, and the words of blessing became a reality. In time, His disciples experienced everything that He had spoken over them. They became what He spoke. The blessing was used to strengthen their lives. Jesus passed on blessings to His disciples, those who were in covenant with Him.

Paul actually opened his letters to each church by speaking blessings upon them. And in 1 Peter 3:8-9, not only does he tell us to put these principles into practice even in the most difficult of situations, but he tells us that we are called to be a people who bless.

Whenever you are struggling to keep a clear heart toward your husband, remember Paul's teachings and the power released through the blessing. Go ahead and speak a blessing over him. If he is acting contrary to the way he should be, call those things that are not as though they were (Romans 4:17). After all, death and life are in the power of the tongue (Prov. 18:21). Prophesy and speak those things into existence!

The words of a [discreet and wise] man's mouth are like deep waters [plenteous and difficult to fathom], and the fountain of skillful and godly wisdom is like a gushing stream [sparkling, fresh, pure, and life-giving]. (Proverbs 18:4 AMP)

Speak life! Call forth the strengths and gifts within your husband. Pronounce and speak a blessing over him. Speak good things! In doing so, something powerful will be released as a result. And remember, 1 Peter 3:9 says that your inheritance is tied to blessing.

Finally, all of you, be of one mind, having compassion for one another, love as brothers, be tenderhearted, be courteous, not returning evil for evil or reviling for reviling, but on the contrary, blessing. Knowing that you were called to this, **that you might inherit a blessing.** (1 Peter 3:8-9 NKJV)

Personally, I am ready to see every plan, purpose, and assignment of the enemy canceled against me, my husband, my marriage, my home, and my family. I am ready to inherit a blessing! What about you?

How have I been handling conflict with my husband?

_____

_____

_____

_____

What gifts, potential, and possibilities do I see within my husband?

_____

_____

_____

_____

Write out a blessing over your husband in the space provided:

_____

_____

_____

_____

_____

_____

_____

_____

_____

_____

Prayer

I speak and pronounce blessings over my husband. When I bless, a blessing comes back to me. According to 1 Peter 3:9, I will inherit a blessing myself when I handle conflict correctly. Every time I handle conflict correctly in my marriage, the enemy is disarmed! His plans are canceled. No weapon formed against my marriage can prosper. I resist the easy and familiar habit of returning negative words with more negative words. Death and life are in the power of my tongue, and I choose to speak life! The words of my mouth are like deep waters. I speak with godly wisdom and my words are like a gushing stream which bring forth sparkling, fresh, pure, and life-giving waters. Give me a vision of what my husband is in Your heart, Oh God, that I might declare it over his life. I am a woman who is called to bless!

PERSONAL REFLECTIONS

_____

_____

_____

_____

_____

_____

_____

_____

_____

_____

_____

_____

_____

_____

_____

_____

_____

_____

_____

Day 19

I Am My Husband's Crown

An excellent wife is the crown of her husband, but she who causes shame is like rottenness in his bones.

Proverbs 12:4 NKJV

A wife can either bring honor and great joy to her husband, or great shame and misery. Here in Proverbs 12:4, the word "excellent" translates "virtuous" and "wife of valor." It is the same Hebrew word *chayil* used in Proverbs 31:10. A virtuous wife is the *crown* of her husband! She is a credit and his honor, his glory and his ornament. She adorns and beautifies his life.

A crown can represent a number of things. The crown is a sign of kingly power. It shows forth a man's position. A husband is the head of his household, a king and a priest of his home. The wife holds up and supports his position with respect and godly submission. A crown also represents joy and gladness.

A virtuous and worthy wife [earnest and strong in character] is a crowning joy to her husband. (Proverbs 12:4 AMP)

Go forth, O daughters of Zion, and see King Solomon with the crown with which his mother crowned him on the day of his wedding, the day of the gladness of his heart. (Song of Solomon 3:11 NKJV)

In Jewish weddings of the first century, the bridegroom wore a crown. This crown was a wreath of fresh garland or flowers worn on the head. It was referred to as a nuptial crown. The custom of Jews and other nations was to put the nuptial crown on the heads of *both* the man and the woman on the marriage day, the day of the gladness of his heart and the day he rejoices over his bride. What a beautiful image from past traditions! It is also an image and reflection of Christ the Bridegroom's love for His bride, the church, and the message of salvation, redemption, and unity. We have a part in putting this gospel message on display as we walk in our role as a virtuous wife, loving, honoring, and even bringing great joy and gladness to the heart of our own husband.

This kind of wife is said to be the best thing in a man's life! She is truly a gift from the Lord.

> House and riches are the inheritance of fathers, but a prudent wife is from the Lord. (Proverbs 19:14 NKJV)

A virtuous wife is more valuable to a man than houses or riches! Houses and riches can be an inheritance passed down from parents but a prudent wife is recognized as being a gift from the Lord Himself. By definition, a prudent wife is one who is "understanding, wise, has insight, makes good decisions, behaves and one who causes her husband to prosper." So important are these characteristics of a prudent and virtuous wife that older, more mature wives were strongly urged to teach and train the younger wives in these very things:

> That they may teach the younger women to be sober, to love their husbands, to love their children, to be discreet, chaste, keepers at home, good, obedient to their own husbands, that the word of God be not blasphemed. (Titus 2:4-5 NKJV)

What really strikes me about these particular verses is the last part of verse five: "...that the word of God be not blasphemed." What does that mean!? I see this same kind of language in Romans 2:24, when

Paul addresses the rulers: "...for the name of God is blasphemed among the Gentiles through you, as it is written." These are strong and cutting words. I do not want to destroy my Christian influence in any way, not through my personal walk or my relationship with my husband. And I certainly do not want reproach to come upon the name of the Lord through me.

The word "blasphemed" means to be "defamed, reviled, to speak reproachfully, dishonored or discredited." Just as a wife's behavior can bring shame to her husband (Proverbs 12:4), it can also bring shame to the word of God. It can dishonor His name. It can harm her own Christian testimony before others, especially unbelievers.

Albert Barnes says this concerning Titus 2:5, "...that the word of God be not blasphemed..."

> That the gospel may not be injuriously spoken of on account of the inconsistent lives of those who profess to be influenced by it. The idea is that religion ought to produce the virtues here spoken of, and that when it does not, it will be reproached as being of no value.

Have you ever thought about it like that? I am talking about your role as a wife. I believe that most of us are careful to not just talk the talk, but to walk the walk, in our daily lives and personal relationship with the Lord... but what about in our marriage relationship...in private... and in public? Do you think of your marriage as a testimony before others? Can others see Christ through your marriage? Do they see Christ through your role as a wife? What is it that they see?

_____

_____

_____

_____

Do I bring honor to God as a wife?

_____

_____

_____

_____

Do I bring honor or dishonor to my husband?

_____

_____

_____

_____

Do I bring joy and gladness to his life?

_____

_____

_____

_____

As a wife, how can I become the crown of my husband?

_____

_____

_____

_____

Prayer

Lord, I am not perfect, but I am consistently growing and developing as a virtuous wife and in that area, along with every area of my life, I desire to bring honor to You. Therefore, I will hold up and support my husband's position in our marriage and home. I will treat him with love, respect and godly submission. I will be like an ornament that beautifies his life, bringing joy and gladness to his heart. I will be to him more valuable than houses and riches. I will be a credit to him, his honor and his glory. I will be my husband's crown.

PERSONAL REFLECTIONS

_____

_____

_____

_____

_____

_____

_____

_____

_____

_____

_____

_____

_____

I Am My Husband's Glory

For a man indeed ought not to cover his head, since he is the image and glory of God; but woman is the glory of man. For man is not from woman, but woman from man. Nor was man created for the woman, but woman for the man.

1 Corinthians 11:7-9 (NKJV)

Before we dive in today, I want you to think of some of your favorite things and jot them down.

What is your favorite food, flower, bird, and animal?

_____

_____

_____

_____

What is your favorite color and your favorite gem or jewel?

_____

_____

_____

_____

What is your favorite place to visit or just dream about visiting?

_____

_____

_____

_____

What are some things that just take your breath away?

_____

_____

_____

_____

For me, my favorite food is chocolate. I can refer to chocolate as food, right? I might occasionally substitute it for a meal. At any rate, it is chocolate that "takes me away." I tend to eat it slowly. When it comes to flowers, some of my favorites are the magnolia, the tiger lily, plumeria, and cherry blossoms. And to me, there is just something about a field full of wild flowers that awakens something glorious on the inside of me. Birds...I love to watch birds. Blue birds, hummingbirds, and woodpeckers are a delight to see on a regular basis. The goldfinch fascinates me with its indescribable grace and beauty. When my eyes catch sight of cardinals from my kitchen window, I immediately stop everything that I am doing. The dishwashing stops. Whatever is cooking on the stove has to wait. I just can't help myself. Their rich red color captures my complete attention. When it comes to animals, giraffes and tigers amaze me. I find the magnificent pattern of spots on the leopard most beautiful. And wild horses are truly something to behold.

Blue is my favorite color in any shade. And I don't even have time to tell you about my favorite gems and stones or the reasons why

I love them. Let me just say that the tanzanite might be the next stone I purchase.

Something as simple as a hike in the woods and a babbling creek does it for me. The sound of the moving waters, the fresh air, the warmth of the sun on my skin, and the peace that I feel is beyond wonderful. One of the places that I have always wanted to visit is Greece. A Mediterranean cruise would be splendid.

I would have to say that a view of the mountains is what takes my breath away. And I never grow tired of the ocean. Never. I have to add that there is nothing like the sight of a beautiful sunset or a sky full of stars on a clear night. Both leave me speechless. These are just some of the things that cause me to be overwhelmed with a sense of wonder and awe. What about you? And what does any of this have to do with our devotional today? I wanted to create an image of glory and spender. Today, I want you to know that *your* beauty and *your* value super exceed all of these magnificent things. *You* are beyond amazing.

You are so special and so beautiful. Do you know how special you are? Do you know how incredibly significant you are? Do you realize how truly valuable you are? You may not always feel very special or beautiful, but you are. You are!

Let's look at our key scripture today:

> For a man indeed ought not to cover his head, since he is the image and glory of God; but **woman is the glory of man**. For man is not from woman, but woman from man. Nor was man created for the woman, but woman for the man. (1 Corinthians 11:7-9 NKJV emphasis the author's)

First of all, our key scriptures make reference to the origin of man and woman. From the very beginning, the way that the woman was created was distinctly different from anything else God had created. The way in which the woman was formed and fashioned was unique when compared to all of creation. And when God created the woman, it was as if He were saving the very BEST for last!

We can go back to Genesis chapter 1 and read how God made the heavens and the earth by speaking them into existence: the sky, sun, moon, stars, planets, land, and seas. He made all of the creatures of the earth. He spoke and it was! Then He created man. When He created man, He created man in His image and after His likeness (Genesis 1:26). Man was set apart from all other created things in that he was created in the image and likeness of God Himself. We find some details concerning the manner in which the man was created in Genesis chapter 2. "The Lord God formed man from the dust of the earth, and breathed the breath of life into his nostrils and man became a living soul." (Genesis 2:7 KJV)

Genesis 1:2 tells us that the earth was without form and void. Darkness covered it. Out of nothing, God spoke and it was. Man, on the other hand, was formed from the dust of the earth. God formed him like clay in a potter's hand. He was fashioned with great love and care. Man was created by God and for God. And being formed in the image and likeness of God, man was to be a reflection of God. Man was created for God's glory!

Then it happened! As magnificent as everything was that God had created, there wasn't anything that could truly satisfy man. As complex and detailed as every other created thing was, nothing was found suitable for him. Though he was surrounded by breathtaking sights and awesome living things, a loneliness still existed within him. When God looked upon all that He created, He said that it was very good. But none of these "very good" things were sufficient for curing man's loneliness or meeting his deeper needs. So God, seeing that there was a need, created the woman. She was the *answer* to the need. She was that one thing that was missing. And she was the one thing that could cure the loneliness. The woman was more breathtaking than the most breathtaking of sights. She was more satisfying than any other created thing that was given to man. She fulfilled a need within the entire picture of all that had been created. Finally, something, someone... *suitable*. It was as if God saved the very BEST for last! And this is the account of the way that she was created:

> So the LORD God caused a deep sleep to fall upon Adam; and while he slept, He took one of his ribs and closed up the flesh at that place. And the rib which the LORD God had taken from the man He made (fashioned, formed) into a woman, and He brought her and presented her to the man. Then Adam said, **"This** is now bone of my bones, and flesh of my flesh; she shall be called Woman, because she was taken out of Man." For this reason a man shall leave his father and his mother, and shall be joined to his wife; and they shall become one flesh. (Genesis 2:21-24 AMP)

The woman was not created in the same manner that any other created thing was, not even the man. She wasn't spoken into existence, created out of nothing. Neither was she formed out of the dust of the earth. She was created in an entirely unique and separate way. She was different. She was special. She was created from life itself. The woman was carefully formed and intricately fashioned in a very personal and loving way. She was truly God's handiwork, taken from man and presented as a *gift* to him. The woman was created with purpose.

She was so magnificent that his heart was fixed upon her. She was so breathtakingly beautiful that the mountains, the seas, the lush valleys, and even the fields covered with wild flowers could not hold a candle to her. Those complex, detailed, colorful birds of the air all fell pale in comparison to her. None of these things measured up to her, not the tiger with its amazing stripes, not even the leopard with its gorgeous spots. Nothing was more beautiful. The amazing sunsets and the clear skies full of stars could not compete. She was stunning. The blooms of the cherry tree and even the fragrant roses had less appeal. His eyes were completely on her. She was more brilliant than diamonds, more valuable than rubies, and more exquisite than emeralds. She was the only created thing that had the capacity to capture and hold his heart. She was an answer. She was a gift. Her value exceeded anything else placed before him.

Maybe you have never thought of yourself as an answer, but you are. You are an answer. Before today, you may have never seen yourself as a gift. You are. You are a gift! You are a remarkable beauty. You are significant and valuable. And you are your husband's glory!

This word "glory" in 1 Corinthians 11:7 is the word *doxa* in the original Greek language and it means "dignity, glory, honor and praise." It also translates "splendor and brightness." We have been discovering that a virtuous wife can bring honor to her husband. She is also an *expression* of his honor. Genesis 1:27 says that both the man and the woman were created in the image and likeness of God. Therefore, they both reflect and represent God. Through each of them individually, the glory of God is made known. And the image and glory of God is displayed most perfectly through a husband and wife together as one.

Knowing that I am an answer, how can I be an answer to some of my husband's deepest needs right now?

_____

_____

_____

_____

Knowing that I am a gift, in what way can I be a gift to him today?

_____

_____

_____

_____

Prayer

Thank You, Lord God my Creator, for today I recognize that I am one of a kind. I am special, significant, full of great purposes, and I make a difference. I am, indeed, valuable. I am an asset to my husband and I am my husband's glory! Let me walk in a true revelation of these things that I might fulfill the very purposes that You have designed me quite on purpose to fulfill. I pray that no woman would have a low self-image of herself for we have been created in the image and likeness of the Almighty God. Help every one of us recognize our high value and high calling, that we might fulfill *every* purpose that You have for us. And help us to see that there are no small purposes and callings among big purposes and callings, but they are ALL significant. Give every one of us a perspective make-over today, that every part of our lives might be transformed. Oh, I sense some change coming, from the way we view ourselves, to the way we walk, talk, live, and shine!

PERSONAL REFLECTIONS

_____

_____

_____

_____

_____

_____

_____

_____

Day 21

I Am a Trophy Wife

Do not let your adornment be merely outward—arranging the hair, wearing gold, or putting on fine apparel—rather let it be the hidden person of the heart, with the incorruptible beauty of a gentle and quiet spirit, which is very precious in the sight of God. For in this manner, in former times, the holy women who trusted in God also adorned themselves, being submissive to their own husbands, as Sarah obeyed Abraham, calling him lord, whose daughters you are if you do good and are not afraid with any terror.

1 Peter 3: 3-5 (NKJV)

You are his trophy wife, not because you look great walking next to him while holding onto his arm, but because of your inner beauty. 1 Peter 3:3 speaks of a woman who has a gentle and quiet spirit.

A gentle and quiet spirit is mild and peaceable. A wife with a gentle and quiet spirit is calm and tranquil. She is agreeable and composed, not easily angered or quick tempered. She does not answer with harsh words. She knows how to respond rather than react. She is humble and not puffed up with pride. A woman who has a gentle and quiet disposition does not create disturbances. She is calm and free from irritability. Quietness actually means "the absence of turmoil."

The Amplified version says that she has "a peaceful spirit, which is not anxious or wrought up." These characteristics are quite the opposite of a disagreeable and contentious wife...

Do I tend to be anxious? Am I easily upset and on edge? If so, why?

_____

_____

_____

_____

While the trophy wife may be very beautiful physically, her real beauty is her inner heart, the regenerated heart. It is of greatest value and to be most admired. It is the gentle and peaceful disposition of a wife that brings the greater benefit and reward to a husband. Having this nature requires us to be controlled by the Spirit rather than our own flesh. In fact, a gentle and quiet spirit is the fruit of the Spirit.

According to our key scripture verse today, a wife who has a gentle and quiet spirit is **precious** in the sight of God. This is the same adjective (*poluteles*) used of the ointment with which Mary anointed Jesus' feet as she broke her alabaster box. May I suggest that your gentle and quiet spirit can be like a precious (*poluteles*) anointing oil being applied to your husband's life? Just a thought…

There were many different uses for the anointing with oil in the Bible. Many Jews anointed themselves with oil daily as a means of refreshing or invigorating their bodies. It was customary to anoint guests with oil to demonstrate hospitality. The anointing with oil had medicinal purposes. Oil was applied to the sick and would also sooth wounds. The oil had calming and healing properties. The leather of one's shield was rubbed with oil to make it supple and fit for use in battle or war. Oil was used to purify the body in the sanctification process. Anointing oil was applied when one was consecrated to a holy or sacred use or purpose. And it was also used to prepare bodies for burial.

Just suppose for one moment that your gentle and quiet spirit could be like an anointing oil, refreshing and invigorating to your husband's soul. Certainly, it can soothe, calm, and even heal his heart. Could it keep him in the kind of condition necessary to win battles? Is it a stretch to believe that it could be of help to him as he walks in the very purposes that God has set him apart for? If there is even a slight hint of truth in that very thought, then Lord let me break open my alabaster box and pour out a gentle and quiet spirit, in all its preciousness, upon my husband's life.

A husband's real interest is his own happiness and when it comes to being happy in his marriage and home, he depends on these characteristics. Your disposition, your character, the way you speak to him, the way you respond to him, and the way you treat him can be like an anointing oil applied to his life. A woman with a gentle and quiet spirit is precious and of great value.

Do I walk in my emotions or do I walk in the Spirit? What characteristics do I exhibit the most?

_____

_____

_____

_____

Do I spend more time on my outward appearance than I do on my inward character?

_____

_____

_____

_____

What can I do to cultivate my inner beauty?

_____

_____

_____

_____

What commitments do I want to make before the Lord today?

_____

_____

_____

_____

Prayer

Lord, I know that a gentle and quiet heart is a heart that has been regenerated. It is evidence that I have been walking in the Spirit instead of my emotions. Help me to spend time in Your presence everyday where I can quiet my heart before You. Abide in me as I abide in You, Lord. Today, I am settling into Your peace, and I will not allow anything to disturb or disrupt that peace. I will walk in Your peace because I walk in the Spirit. I have the fruit of the Spirit because the Spirit of God lives in me. I am in a constant and continual state of growth. Continue to transform my heart each day, Lord. Allow the inner beauty of Christ to come forth and let it be precious. May it be as an expensive anointing oil poured out on the one I love. May the inner beauty of my heart become my husband's trophy.

Personal Reflections

Day 22

I Am Strong and Graceful

She girds herself with strength, and strengthens her arms. Strength and honor are her clothing. She shall rejoice in time to come.

Proverbs 31:17, 25 (NKJV)

Having a gentle and quiet spirit does not mean that you are shy, timid and weak. The Proverb 31 wife exhibits honorable behavior, but she is anything but timid and weak!

She may be the weaker vessel but she is no weakling. This strength is literally translated as "boldness, might and power." The strengthening of her arms that verse seventeen speaks of actually translates "to be alert, courageous, steadfastly minded, and to prevail." She is strong in the Lord and equipped to handle whatever life throws at her. She is able to bear up under pressure, trials and tribulations. This inner strength is what causes her to persevere. This strength and honor is her clothing. It has become part of her character.

> She girds herself with strength [spiritual, mental, and physical fitness for her God-given task] and makes her arms strong and firm. (Proverbs 31:17 AMP)

Can one wear strength and gentleness at the same time? Is it possible to gird myself with strength, boldness and power, while I am adorned with gentleness and a quiet spirit? The answer is yes! There is so much on the inside of you and me that if we can just learn to tap into it, we will prevail every time. God has given us everything that we need for a life of godliness. It is in you. Don't think for one moment that you cannot be all that God has called you to be as a wife. You can and you will become the wife God desires you to be.

> Grace and peace be multiplied to you in the knowledge of God and of Jesus our Lord, **as His divine power has given to us all things that pertain to life and godliness,** through the knowledge of Him who called us by glory and virtue, by which have been given to us exceedingly great and precious promises, that through these you may be partakers of the divine nature, having escaped the corruption that is in the world because of sinful desire. (2 Peter 1:2-4 ESV)

Do I realize that God has given me all things that pertain to my life and all the things pertaining to godliness? Yes, He is calling me to be a virtuous wife, and He has given me what I need in order to become just that. He promised me that I can be a partaker of His divine nature!

A Proverbs 31 wife is a virtuous wife and a mighty woman of valor. Her footing is firm. She is solid and grounded in Christ, immovable and unshakable. She can handle every one of her God-given tasks with confidence. She is capable.

> A capable, intelligent, and virtuous woman—who is he who can find her? She is far more precious than jewels and her value is far above rubies or pearls. (Proverbs 31:10 AMP)

The Amplified translation actually uses the word capable along with virtuous. **Capable – having the ability, fitness, or quality necessary to do or achieve a specified thing.**

A wife does it all. She wears many hats and wears them all well. She adorns herself with a gentle and quiet spirit. She is clothed with strength, courage, and boldness. She is strong *and* graceful.

A woman's wardrobe is found hanging in her closet. Most likely she has an outfit for every occasion: a coat for a chilly day, a dress for an important or formal event, shoes to match every outfit, and accessories galore. If it is a hot day, she puts on something light and airy. If it is a lazy day, she dresses in something comfortable. She dresses herself accordingly.

I am getting ready to go on vacation with my family to Myrtle Beach. I find myself without a decent bathing suit, and I am going to have to purchase one. I have needed to buy one for quite some time. We do that. I mean, we as women go without some things we need sometimes. I assure you, though, that God has not left us without what we need to gird ourselves and dress ourselves in any given situation. He has given us everything we need for life and godliness.

In a spiritual sense, our closet is full. Our wardrobe is complete. We have just what we need, just when we need it. Throughout scripture, we are told to "take off" and "put on" a number of things. We are told to take off the old man and put on the new man. We are told to put on truth, righteousness, peace, faith, and salvation. We are to clothe ourselves with tender mercies, kindness, meekness, and longsuffering. We are to put on love, put on Christ Jesus, and put on the garment of praise for the spirit of heaviness. As godly wives we can adorn ourselves with a gentle and quiet spirit. We can gird ourselves with strength and honor. Courage and a steadfast mind belong to us. We can wear it all and wear it well.

As a child of the Most High God, you are not lacking anything. As a wife, you are perfectly capable. What will you dress yourself in today?

_____

_____

_____

_____

How often have I felt that I just can't measure up? How often have I felt that my best is never good enough?

_____

_____

_____

_____

Have I been attempting all things in my own power and strength?

_____

_____

_____

_____

Have I been a partaker of His divine nature?

_____

_____

_____

_____

Prayer

Lord, I am so thankful that I can be a partaker of Your divine nature. You have given me all things that pertain to life, my life. You have given me all things that pertain to godliness. I can be a godly wife because of Christ who dwells within me. I have the ability to tackle every one of my God-given tasks. Today, I put on Christ, for it is through Christ, the One who strengthens me, that I can do *all* things.

PERSONAL REFLECTIONS

I Am a Woman Who Fears the Lord

Charm is deceitful and beauty is passing,
but a woman who fears the Lord, she shall be praised.
Proverbs 31:30 (NKJV)

What does it mean to fear the Lord? The fear of the Lord, as used in Proverbs 31:30, is an attitude of respect and reverence. This kind of fear has everything to do with awe and wonder.

John J. Parsons says that the fear of the Lord "includes the idea of wonder, amazement, mystery, astonishment, gratitude, admiration, and even worship...The fear of the Lord includes an overwhelming sense of the glory, worth, and beauty of the One true God." This kind of fear is the highest kind. It is "profound reverence for life that comes from rightly seeing" and it "discerns the presence of God in all things."

Am I filled with awe, wonder, and amazement as I think upon the Lord? When it comes to the Lord, does astonishment, gratitude, admiration, and worship fill my heart? Do I discern the presence of God in all things? Open my spiritual eyes, Lord, that I might be a woman who is always and forever rightly seeing!

The Proverbs 31 wife is a woman who walks in the fear of the Lord. She has a deep reverence for God. Her identity in the Lord is her most attractive quality. It is the true secret of how she is able to successfully fulfill her role of being a wife. Proverbs 31:30 says that she shall be praised. It is true that she is worthy of praise and to be commended; however, if there is anything praiseworthy about her, it is the Lord's work in her life. It is the reason for her excellence.

Proverbs 9:10 tells us that the fear of the Lord is the beginning of wisdom. The Proverbs 31 wife is wise. Christ is the very foundation on which she builds. She is grounded in her faith. She regards the Lord as holy and His precepts as trustworthy. The Proverbs 31 wife understands that while charm can be misleading and beauty may fade, God's Word will never pass away. Many things around her may change, but God is the God who changes not. He is the same yesterday, today, and forever.

Proverbs 8:13 tells us that to fear the Lord is to hate evil, and that she does. It is the fear of the Lord that keeps her from walking in sin and error. Her virtue is of great value in the sight of God and her spouse.

> In the fear of the LORD there is strong confidence, and His children will have a place of refuge. (Proverbs 14:26 NKJV)

The Proverbs 31 wife may be described as capable, and she certainly is. However, she recognizes that her confidence is not in her own ability, but in the Lord's ability. It is upon Him that she truly depends. She is completely aware of how much she needs the Lord in her everyday life. She draws near to Him. She has made Him her sanctuary.

> The secret [of the sweet, satisfying companionship] of the Lord have they who fear (revere and worship) Him, and He will show them His covenant and reveal to them its [deep, inner] meaning. (Psalm 25:14 AMPC)

She is whole, complete, and fulfilled, not because of her relationship with her spouse, but because of her relationship with Christ. It is Christ who fills her and satisfies her. He gives her the desires of her heart. He has placed every one of them within her because she reverently and worshipfully fears Him!

He will fulfill the desire of those who fear Him; He also will hear their cry and save them. (Psalm 145:19 NKJV)

The Proverbs 31 wife has no need to be afraid of anything that she may encounter on her journey. She need not fear man, trials, nor failure itself. She holds fast to the promises of God.

The angel of the Lord encamps all around those who fear Him, and delivers them. (Psalm 34:7 NKJV)

And His mercy is on those who fear Him from generation to generation. (Luke 1:50 NKJV)

Oh, how great is Your goodness, which You have laid up for those who fear You, which You have prepared for those who trust in You in the presence of the sons of men! (Psalm 31:19 NKJV)

Behold, the Lord's eye is upon those who fear Him [who revere and worship Him with awe], who wait for Him and hope in His mercy and loving-kindness, to deliver them from death and keep them alive in famine. Our inner selves wait [earnestly] for the Lord; He is our Help and our Shield. (Psalm 33:18-20 AMPC)

His protection, His mercy, provision, and care are promised and demonstrated to those who fear Him. The Lord has laid up and reserved good things for those who fear Him. The fear of the Lord leads to life.

The fear of the Lord **leads to life**; then one rests content, untouched by trouble. (Proverbs 19:23 NIV emphasis the author's)

This life is the abundant life that John 10:10 speaks of. It is a full, rich life, one that is worth living. Albert Barnes says that this abundance is "not absolutely essential to life, but that which is superadded to make life happy. They shall not merely have life—simple, bare existence— but shall have all those superadded things which are needful to make life eminently blessed and happy."

> The fear of the LORD is **a fountain of life**, to turn one away from the snares of death. (Proverbs 14:27 NKJV)

Proverbs 14:27 says that the fear of the Lord is a fountain of life. It is a source or wellspring of life! Matthew Henry describes it as "an ever-flowing spring of comfort and joy; it is a fountain *of life,* yielding constant pleasure and satisfaction to the soul, joys that are pure and fresh, are life to the soul, and quench its thirst, and can never be drawn dry; it is a *well of living water,* that is springing up to, and is the earnest of, eternal life. True happiness and real contentment flows out of a life which fears the Lord."

And Proverbs 19:23 confirms that the one who has this kind of life rests content and absolutely untouched by trouble.

Have you been resting content? Is your life full and rich, or are you experiencing only a bare existence? Are you really living?

_____

_____

_____

_____

Do you hate sin and evil?

_____

_____

_____

Do you deeply respect and revere the Lord?

_____

_____

_____

_____

Prayer

Lord, I am amazed by You. You are an awesome God. I am full of gratitude when I think of who You are and what You have done. Help me in the area of "rightly seeing." Remind me that my entire identity is found in You. If I am overwhelmed by anything at all, let it be that I am overwhelmed by You, overwhelmed by Your love, overwhelmed by Your goodness, and overwhelmed by Your presence. Today, I choose to make You my sanctuary. I want to know that sweet, satisfying companionship found within my relationship with You. Create in me a deeper and greater reverence for You. Allow me to walk in abundant life and enjoy the superadded things, the things which are needful to making my life eminently blessed and happy and the things that do not pass away. I thank You that I can experience true happiness and real contentment in my life, in my marriage, and in my home. I am a woman who fears the Lord.

PERSONAL REFLECTIONS

_____

_____

_____

_____

_____

_____

_____

_____

_____

_____

_____

_____

_____

_____

_____

_____

_____

_____

_____

_____

_____

_____

_____

_____

Day 24

I Am Blessed

*Her children rise up and call her **blessed** (happy, fortunate, and to be envied); and her husband boasts of and praises her, [saying], Many daughters have done virtuously, nobly, and well [with the strength of character that is steadfast in goodness], but you excel them all.*

Proverbs 31:28-29 (AMPC)

What does it really mean to be blessed? Am I blessed? Are you blessed? The Proverb's wife was blessed. Apparently it was evident. Even her children could see and recognize that she was blessed.

Blessed is everyone who fears the LORD, who walks in His ways. (Psalm 128:1 NKJV)

First of all, she is in a blessed state because she fears the Lord. When you read this scripture, it is as if the Lord is actually pronouncing a blessing over those who fear Him. He calls them blessed! I love what Matthew Henry says about this: "Blessed is everyone that fears the Lord, whoever he may be; in every nation he that fears God and works righteousness is accepted of him, and therefore is blessed whether he be high or low, rich or poor…"

That makes you rethink what it means to truly be blessed, doesn't it? Don't ever make the mistake of judging whether you are blessed or not blessed by the present circumstances surrounding your life. Do you fear the Lord? Do you walk in His ways? If so, God Himself calls you blessed.

The husband in Proverbs 31 did not boast about his wife because of the good times that they were experiencing or the favorable circumstances of the season they were in. Real life is not always a bowl of cherries. Circumstances change. He boasted about the strength of character he witnessed within her that remained steady and constant. It was this virtue that he counted praiseworthy. She was blessed and she was a blessing. She was a blessing to him. She was unlike any other woman in his life. She had his heart.

> Her children rise up and call her blessed (**happy, fortunate, and to be envied**); and her husband boasts of and praises her, [saying], Many daughters have done virtuously, nobly, and well [with the strength of character that is steadfast in goodness], but you excel them all. (Proverbs 31:28-29)

Why is she happy, considered fortunate, and to be envied?

The word "blessed" means "favored, made happy and prosperous." She has God's favor in her life. There is a deep spiritual happiness that she is enjoying as well. Her relationship with her husband and children brings her great joy.

When I think of the word prosperous, I think about 3 John 1:2, which says, "Beloved, I pray that you may prosper in all things and be in health, just as your soul prospers." (NKJV) Many people associate prosperity with financial blessing. Did you know that you can prosper in many different ways? According to this verse, you can even prosper in your soul. Your soul is your heart, your mind, your will, and emotions. Let's face it, if you are healthy in your body but you are a wreck in your soul, then how will you be able to enjoy your good physical health and a long life? And if you have wealth yet your soul is low, how will you enjoy your riches? Allow the Lord to bring prosperity first to your soul!

Here in 3 John 1:2, the word "prosper" in the original Greek language is the word *euodoō*. It is a compound word from *eu*, meaning "good" and also the word *hodos*, meaning "the way, a road or route, a journey, highway, and distance." To prosper translates "to help on the road, a prosperous journey, and to succeed in reaching."

There are times when we, as wives, grow weary. Sometimes we are just plain tired from the many responsibilities we juggle day in and day out. At times you may wonder how in the world will you ever be able to go the distance! Don't fret! You are a woman who fears the Lord and walks in His ways. He will help you along the road. He is with you on your journey. You will succeed in reaching your potential and fulfilling God's purposes for your life. It is the Lord who helps you to succeed! You are favored. You are prosperous, made happy, fortunate, and to be envied. You are blessed! You may not always feel blessed. You may not always see the evidence of a blessed life, but God calls you blessed.

There is a time to sow. Then there is a time to enjoy the harvest of all of your laboring, all of your prayers, and all of your faithfulness. You pour into your marriage and into your home. This may very well be the season that you are in right now. It is a time of sowing. You may not always see the rewards right away, but God tells us in His Word that as long as the earth remains, seed time and harvest shall not cease. Whatever we sow, we will also reap. It is a spiritual principle, so keep sowing! Your harvest shall surely come.

> For you shall eat [the fruit] of the labor of your hands; happy (blessed, fortunate, enviable) shall you be, and it shall be well with you. (Psalm 128:2 AMPC)

A Proverbs 31 wife is blessed today. She is blessed in every season and circumstance of her life. She is blessed now and forever more. She is blessed in her marriage. She is blessed in her home. She is blessed in the city and she is blessed in the field. She is blessed going in and coming out. In time, she will enjoy the fruit of all of her labor because she faints not. She will indeed reap a harvest because she does not give up.

Let us not become weary in doing good, for at the proper time we will reap a harvest if we do not give up. (Galatians 6:9 NIV)

Do you recognize how blessed you really are?

_____

_____

_____

_____

Are you prospering in your soul?

_____

_____

_____

_____

What have you been sowing in your marriage and in your home?

_____

_____

_____

_____

What kind of harvest are you expecting?

_____

_____

_____

_____

Prayer

Lord, thank You for Your countless blessings that You have bestowed upon me. Forgive me for the times that I have not recognized them or been grateful. I am happy and most fortunate! Today my prayer is that I would continually prosper in my soul. My prayer is that I would truly be a blessing to my husband and my children. In my marriage, make me a blessing to him unlike any other person in his life. Continue to bless me. Bless my marriage and bless my home. Bless it now, Lord, in new and even greater ways, I pray.

PERSONAL REFLECTIONS

_____

_____

_____

_____

_____

_____

_____

_____

_____

_____

_____

_____

_____

_____

_____

_____

_____

_____

_____

_____

_____

_____

_____

_____

_____

_____

_____

_____

_____

_____

_____

_____

_____

_____

Day 25

I Am A Fruitful Vine Within My House

Blessed is everyone who fears the Lord, who walks in His ways. For you shall eat the labor of your hands, you shall be happy and it shall be well with you. **Your wife shall be like a fruitful vine in the very heart of your house,** *your children like olive plants all around your table. Behold, thus shall the man be blessed who fears the Lord.*

Psalm 128:1-4 (NKJV)

The Proverbs 31 wife is a woman who fears the Lord. She walks in His ways and keeps His commandments. Because she regularly conforms to the Lord's will, she thrives and bears fruit in every area of her life. In her home, she is like a fruitful vine. She is honored and respected by her children. Her husband has reason to praise her. Their home is a healthy home. It is healthy and thriving whether circumstances are high or low, rich or poor.

How can a wife be like a fruitful vine within her house?

To be fruitful means to grow, increase, and bring forth fruit. Clearly our Proverbs model wife was fruitful. We find her in Proverbs 31 being quite productive. She was busy accomplishing many things, including ministry to the poor, yet her priority was that of taking care of the needs of her own household, her family.

You see, a wife should be like a fruitful vine in the very heart of her home. She may be an amazing woman who accomplishes many great things in and out of her home, but her first and best work should be done within her own home: the best of her time, the best of her energy, the best of her creativity and resourcefulness, and the best of her love. She may be a busy woman, but her chief usefulness and her first calling is within the building of her own home.

The King James Version of our key verse today uses the words, "Thy wife shall be as a fruitful vine by the sides of thine house." This creates some very beautiful imagery. First of all, let's note that she is not found on the roof, for she is not above her husband. She is not the head. Neither do we see her near the ground, for she is not under her husband's feet, but she is at his side.

In the East, it was a common custom of Jews to train a vine along the sides of a house. The vine actually had its root within the house, but it would grow and spread along the sides of the house. This kind of vine would cleave to the side of the house and it would bear fruit. It was pliable and grew where it was directed. There, on the side of the house, it grew, it thrived, and it flourished.

There were a number of purposes for training a vine to grow and spread along the sides of the house. The vine would provide shade and comfort from the heat. It would also let in winter sunlight and warmth. It could protect and defend the house against the forces of winds, rain, and even thieves. The vine had good exposure for fruit right where it was planted. It was also an ornament, beautifying the home.

The word "vine" in Psalm 128:3 translates "to bend; a vine (as twining)." That is an interesting translation in that we have been learning that a wife is to adapt herself to her husband. Bending and adapting certainly carry the same idea.

Like the illustration of the fruitful, twining vine along the side of a house, a wife is called alongside her husband. She cleaves to him. He is her support. They are intertwined as one and move forward together. She is also an individual with her own thoughts, feelings, desires, and interests, but her roots always remain within her home. As she walks in her role as his wife, she grows and she bears fruit. Not only does she bear children who are like olive shoots around the table, but everything she puts her hands and heart to bears good fruit.

Proverbs 31:18 tells us that "she tastes and sees that her gain from her work [with and for God} is good."

She is a comforter to her husband. She is also his advocate and his backer. This wife of valor often places herself between the arrows of the enemy and her husband and children. She is a watchman who keeps the enemy at bay. No thief will be permitted to come in and steal what she and her husband have together. She recognizes that the Lord's blessings are upon her life. She does not take that for granted. Her children and husband count her as a blessing. She is the beautiful ornament of their home. And her home has become one that is healthy and thriving. She is a fruitful vine within her house!

Is my first and best work done in my home? Is it there that I give the best of my time, energy, creativity, resourcefulness, and love?

_____

_____

_____

_____

In all of the many things I do outside of my home, do my roots remain in the heart of my home?

_____

_____

_____

_____

Am I pliable?

_____

_____

_____

_____

Do I believe that my best exposure for producing fruit is right where I am planted?

_____

_____

_____

_____

Prayer

Lord, help me to continue to put down solid roots in the soil of my home and keep it my priority. Help me to remember that it is my husband that supports the root system within that soil. I dedicate myself to giving the best of who I am in the heart of my home. Cause me to grow, increase, and bring forth fruit in every area of my life and especially within my marriage. Make me a fruitful vine within my house.

PERSONAL REFLECTIONS

Day 26

I Am a Watchman

She watches over the ways of her household,
and does not eat the bread of idleness.

Proverbs 31:27 (NKJ)

The Proverbs 31 wife watches over the ways of her family and her entire household. The word "ways" literally means "their coming and going, their activities, and all that is happening." You might say that all of us make it our business to know what is going on in the lives of those who live in our own household. This watching that the Proverbs 31 wife was doing, however, carried a great responsibility and purpose, one which we will do well to learn from. The word "watches" in Proverbs 31:27 is the Hebrew word *tsâphâh*, and it creates an image of the Old Testament watchman on the wall. *Tsâphâh* means "to lean forward, to peer into the distance, to watch closely, to keep watch, survey, guard" and it translates to "watchman."

Great ancient cities had thick walls around the entire city for protection, cities like Babylon and Jerusalem. Watchmen were guards who were assigned to specific territories. They would stand upon the walls and in the towers to look out upon the land. Their main task was to look out for any signs of disturbance or schemes and activity of the enemy. It was their job to report anything suspicious to the commander. If there was any threat at all, the gates were shut. If they saw any sign of an army approaching, they sounded the warning and the people prepared for battle.

In Nehemiah chapter 4, we can read about the rebuilding of the wall in Jerusalem. When the wall was being rebuilt, there were still gaps in the wall that were referred to as "exposed places." The watchmen were on guard and took extra care to protect those weak or exposed places.

As wives, one of our roles is to watch over our household, our assigned territory. When it comes to our marriages, we need to be a watchman looking out with spiritual eyes, discerning the enemy's schemes and activity. We must go to battle in the spirit with prayer. It is vital that we take our position and exercise our authority over the enemy. As we are building our homes and our marriages, we must take special care to guard the exposed places or weak areas.

During the process of building our homes and growing a good, strong marriage, there are areas that we are still working on. These areas are currently vulnerable and the enemy is looking for a way to attack the weakest part. He desires to find a gap so big that he can get in and wreak havoc. He is truly your adversary and opponent. With a staggering 50 percent divorce rate among married couples, unbelievers and believers alike, it is clear that the enemy desires to destroy marriage and the family unit as a whole. It is your job as the watchman to sound the warning and shut the gate. Give him no access. Let nothing disturb the love, peace, and unity in your growing marriage.

> Be sober, be vigilant; because your adversary the devil walks about like a roaring lion, seeking whom he may devour.
> (1 Peter 5:8 NKJV)

It is time to be alert and aware, sober and vigilant. It is time to recognize just what is really happening when any form of chaos comes into our homes. We need to discern just what the enemy is trying to accomplish. It is his plan to divide and conquer. Take your post. Survey and guard what belongs to you.

In ancient times, watchtowers were placed overlooking the fields. When the crops were ripening and it was close to the time of harvest, it was vital that a watchman was present to guard the field from animals and even thieves. The entire community's food and sustenance was at stake. You have been working and sowing into your marriage and home. Let no enemy come in and steal, kill, or destroy what you have been laboring for. The harvest belongs to you. Therefore you, by all means, should enjoy its fruit.

We see from our key verse today that the Proverbs wife is not lax concerning these things. She watches over the ways of her household, **and does not eat the bread of idleness. She is not slack when it comes to watching over the well-being of her marriage and her home.** Neither is she lazy nor careless when it comes to guarding that which the Lord has entrusted to her. She does not neglect her role as a watchman.

Webster's definition of idleness is "lacking worth or basis." You, friend, have been discovering your worth, value, and significance as a wife. Your role is vital. You are becoming more determined than ever to have the marriage that God intends for you to have. It is time to secure the parameters, preventing any evil from getting in. Though the enemy prowls around like a roaring lion, seeking whom he may devour, he may **not** devour *your* marriage or home! Though he looks for an opportunity, you will give him none. You are a woman devoted to great purpose. You are not only devoted to the physical well-being of your household, but also the spiritual well-being. You are concerned with the total well-being of your entire household and like the Proverbs wife, you too will enjoy the fruit of your labor.

Ephesians 6:12 clearly tells us that our struggles are not against flesh and blood but against spiritual forces of darkness. My husband is not my enemy. He is not my adversary or my opponent. We are on the same team! We must always remember who our real enemy is. Woman of God, if there must be a battle, then fight! But make sure that all of your fighting is directed against the spiritual forces of darkness. Take the spiritual authority that God has given you, and take it into the right battlefield. Pray. Fast. Take your place on the wall.

Keep a cool head. Stay alert. The Devil is poised to pounce, and would like nothing better than to catch you napping. Keep your guard up. You're not the only ones plunged into these hard times. It's the same with Christians all over the world. So keep a firm grip on the faith. The suffering won't last forever. It won't be long before this generous God who has great plans for us in Christ—eternal and glorious plans they are!—will have you put together and on your feet for good. He gets the last word; yes, he does. (1 Peter 5:8-11 MSG)

How have I been viewing the battles that I have faced or am now facing within my marriage and home?

_____

_____

_____

_____

Have I been a vigilant watchman or have I been slack and careless in this area?

_____

_____

_____

_____

What have I allowed to come into my marriage and into my home? What gates need to be shut?

_____

_____

_____

_____

What are the weak, vulnerable, or exposed places in my marriage at this time? How can I guard and protect these areas?

_____

_____

_____

_____

What can I do to secure the perimeter of my marriage and my home?

_____

_____

_____

_____

My own Prayer of Commitment:

_____

_____

_____

_____

PERSONAL REFLECTIONS

Day 27

My Oil Keeps Burning

She rises while it is yet night and gets [spiritual] food for her household and assigns her maids their tasks....She tastes and sees that her gain from work [with and for God] is good; her lamp goes not out, but it burns on continually through the night [of trouble, privation, or sorrow, warning away fear, doubt, and distrust].

Proverbs 31:15, 18 AMP

In verse 18, the virtuous wife's lamp does not go out, but it burns on continuously through the night. This gives us the impression that she works into the night. This is most likely true—after all, a woman's work is never done! It is usually the wife and mother who is the last one in bed at night and the first one to get up in the morning. We have learned from Proverbs 31 that this wife is not idle and she works tirelessly. However, the Amplified version gives us an even clearer picture. Night here is described as a night season of "trouble, hardship, sorrow, fear, doubt and distrust." The original Hebrew word used for night in this text translates "adversity."

In verse 15, we get a glimpse of just what kind of activity she is partaking in during the night season. She is getting spiritual food for herself and her family. She is up in the night hours getting into God's presence. She is seeking God. She is in His Word and in prayer. Her lamp may be burning in the natural, but it is also burning in the spirit as well.

In the natural, oil lamps were used at the time these scriptures were written. Oil was used for the lighting and burning of lamps. This olive oil was highly valued. The process of getting the oil from olives is quite an interesting process itself. The olive trees were literally beaten and shaken till the olives fell to the ground. The olives were then soaked in water to clean them and purge them of their bitterness. Next they were crushed in the oil press to extract their oil. Sometimes they were crushed or trodden out by the feet.

Maybe some of the circumstances that you have walked through have left you feeling beaten and shaken. Maybe your heart has been knocked to the ground a time or two. Have you been crushed? Have you been pressed on every side? Have there been a few occasions when someone walked all over you with their words or actions? Remember, the oil that was pressed out from this process was highly valued. The process had a way of purifying the oil. A cleansing took place as part of the process. As the olives were soaked, a purging took place. They were purged of their bitterness. The bitter quality of the olive was removed in the soaking process.

There is a process that will cleanse us when we are walking through a night season of adversity in our lives. It's called soaking in His presence. The Proverbs 31 wife was a woman who was continually seeking God through His Word, prayer, and sitting in His presence. She communed with God in good times and in troubled times. This one thing made her ready and capable to fulfill her role and all the related responsibilities. Staying in His presence enabled her to be virtuous and courageous. It was through this process that she was shaped into the kind of woman that was worthy of the praises of her children, her husband, and those in the community. And it was this soaking that prepared her to handle any and every adversity that she would ever walk through in her life without becoming bitter.

To purge means to clear of impurities and to remove toxins. Even in a spiritual sense, to purify means "to purify, deliver, and remove anything that would defile." It means "to unburden and make free from guilt." Although here in this text, the oil itself does not represent us, the believer, I want us to consider this particular process because this process looks a lot like the *night seasons* that we walk through. And it is during the process of getting pressed on every side that we can become bitter. It is during the crushing events in our lives that the enemy would like for us to withdraw from God and take in every negative thought and emotion which desires to assault the soul.

Seasons of difficulty have the potential to make us bitter or better. It is the Lord's intention and plan that we be made better. We are made better when we remain in His presence.

Oil in the Bible is most often a symbol of the Holy Spirit. Lamps can symbolize vessels that are to be filled and lit. The Proverbs wife understood the importance of continually being filled with the Spirit of God. I want to talk about this some more, but first let's take some time to reflect on just how to be cleansed from even the residue of night seasons. Let's rid ourselves of any bitter qualities that have settled upon our hearts. Spend some time in God's presence right now and allow Him to soak and saturate you in a way that unburdens, purifies, delivers, and heals you today.

How much time daily do I spend alone with the Lord, soaking in His presence?

_____

_____

_____

_____

Do I run *to* Him or *from* Him when life is painful?

_____

_____

_____

_____

What events in my marriage have caused me to become bitter?

_____

_____

_____

_____

Am I ready to be purged from any and all bitterness in my heart?

_____

_____

_____

_____

Prayer

Lord, I soak in Your presence today. Rid me of any bitter quality that is in my heart and life. Remove anything that would defile me. Purge me from every toxin. Purify my heart. Unburden me and make me free. Deliver me and heal me. Wash me, cleanse me, and fill me. I give You permission right now, Lord, to take everything in my life that the enemy meant for harm, and use it for my good and Your glory. Make me better and not bitter. Fill me with the oil of Your Spirit and keep me burning for You. Let my lamp continue to burn in good times and in times of trouble. Let it burn in the daylight and in the night seasons alike. My oil shall burn continually.

PERSONAL REFLECTIONS

_____

_____

_____

_____

_____

_____

_____

_____

_____

_____

_____

_____

_____

_____

_____

_____

_____

_____

_____

_____

_____

_____

Day 28

My Lamp Stays Lit

She rises while it is yet night and gets [spiritual] food for her household and assigns her maids their tasks. She tastes and sees that her gain from work [with and for God] is good; **her lamp goes not out, but it burns on continually through the night [of trouble, privation, or sorrow, warning away fear, doubt, and distrust].**

Proverbs 31: 15,18 (AMP)

Oil in the Bible most often represents the Holy Spirit and lamps represent vessels. When I think of oil and lamps, I immediately think about the parable of the ten virgins. You remember the parable of the ten virgins.

When it was announced that the bridegroom was coming, five of the ten virgins did not have enough oil to keep their lamps burning. These five virgins were referred to as *foolish*. The five foolish virgins asked the other five to give them some of their oil. The other five virgins were referred to as *wise* virgins because not only did they keep their lamps burning, but they were prepared. Apparently they made sure that they remained in frequent contact with their source of oil. They regularly visited their supplier so that they had ample supply.

Now it was night when the announcement came that the bridegroom was coming. The bridegroom was on his way to get the virgins and take them to the wedding supper. They would need these lamps to light their way as they followed him.

The wise virgins suggested that the foolish virgins go and buy more oil of their own. Until now, the foolish virgins had seemed unconcerned about their future. They had not prepared. It seems that during the bridegroom's delay in coming, they had become complacent while they waited. It appears that they began to neglect their visits to their source of oil. They simply were not ready.

When asked for some of their oil, the wise virgins replied by saying no. The bridegroom arrived while the foolish, unprepared virgins were on their way to buy more oil. They were in a scramble to get their act together at the very last minute.

The wise virgins had plenty of oil and their lamps did not go out. They went with the bridegroom. They went right into the wedding feast and the door was shut. The foolish virgins arrived too late and were not permitted to enter in.

A relationship with the Lord cannot be borrowed. Neither can a person's character. A relationship with the Lord is developed and one's character is shaped and built through a process.

A woman who is a vessel for the Lord, who is continually filled with the Holy Spirit and keeps herself burning for Him, will be prepared to handle any and every season in her life, including night seasons. Come trouble, come hardship and lack, she remains strong and secure. Though sorrow, heartache, and pain may inevitably touch her life, she is not overcome by it. Her character and steady heart have been shaped by her time spent in God's presence. The light of this kind of oil, according to verse 18, warns away fear, doubt, and distrust.

The Proverbs wife had a continual walk with the Lord that made her ready and able to handle any amount of adversity that came her way with an amazing inner strength. She was ready and prepared to navigate the ups and downs of her journey. She was ready to run the race and finish her course. And she was ready for eternity.

The Proverbs 31 wife may have been busy with the tasks and responsibilities of her life, but she was never too busy to nurture her relationship with Christ. She was not too busy to sit in His presence and receive a continual flow of His Spirit. And she was, therefore, empowered in *every* area of her life, including her marriage.

What about you? Do you find yourself blindsided and unprepared for adversity when it comes?

_____

_____

_____

_____

Have you become complacent? Have you been neglecting or nurturing your relationship with the Lord?

_____

_____

_____

_____

Have you kept your lamp lit and burning? Do you continually visit your source?

_____

_____

_____

_____

How full is your lamp right now?

_____

_____

_____

_____

Are there any new commitments that you would like to make today?

_____

_____

_____

_____

Prayer

Lord, today the prayer in my heart is simply the words to A. Sevison's hymn, "Give Me Oil in My Lamp."

> Give me oil in my lamp, keep me burning.
> Give me oil in my lamp, I pray.
> Give me oil in my lamp, keep me burning.
> Keep me burning till the break of day.

Continually fill me with fresh oil, Lord! Father God, I am determined to nurture my relationship with You. You alone are my source. And I declare today that my oil keeps burning and my lamp stays lit!

PERSONAL REFLECTIONS

_____

_____

_____

_____

_____

_____

_____

_____

_____

_____

_____

_____

_____

_____

_____

_____

_____

_____

_____

_____

_____

_____

_____

Day 29

I Excel

Many daughters have done virtuously, nobly, and well [with the strength of character that is steadfast in goodness], but you excel them all.

Proverbs 31:29 (AMPC)

According to Proverbs 31:29, many women have been virtuous and noble. Many women have done well. Although there are many who possess a certain strength of character, there is something about the Proverbs 31 wife that excels above the rest.

The word "excel" comes from the word "excellent." By definition it means "to be exceptionally good at or proficient in an area, outstanding, to surpass in some respect; achievements or accomplishments, to be highly skilled, to go beyond, to be distinguishable, and to shine."

What is it about the Proverbs 31 wife that distinguished her from the larger group? Could it be that she had gone beyond what the culture of her age had set as an acceptable standard when it came to the role of a wife, marriage, and the making of a home?

What about our culture today? Is there a clear standard when it comes to the sanctity of marriage, or are the lines becoming more and more blurred every day? What about the standard in which we, as wives, are to live by? Does our culture reinforce God's holy standards or have the unholy things become very acceptable and commonplace? I dare you to become a Proverbs 31 wife and raise the standard in your generation. Go beyond what is common. Cultivate a marriage and a home that is uncommon in this age, one that shines and reflects God's holiness and His glory.

Excel in this particular text is the Hebrew word *âlâh* and it translates "to perfect, to work, to get up, rise up, to ascend, to begin to spring forth, shoot forth, increase, stir up, and leap."

We see then that the scripture is not saying that the Proverbs wife is perfect. Instead, she is a wife who is in a process of perfecting the skills that God has given her. If she is excellent at anything, it is because she works at it. It is just that important to her.

Still, there is something about this Proverbs 31 wife that is distinguishable from the group majority. Could it be that, at some point in her life, she made a decision to get up from her past defeats? Could it be that she just kept rising up no matter what came her way to discourage her and put her down? Was it her willingness to submit to God's plan and process that caused her to spring up, and even shoot forth, as a woman ever-increasing in every area of her life? Was it her sincere desire to truly be the wife that God had called her to be that put her on the path of becoming the one we refer to today as our biblical role model?

These are good questions. Proverbs 31 describes the many characteristics of this model wife, but it does not describe her journey of becoming the woman who we admiringly read about now. For each of us, the journey may look very different.

There is no doubt the Proverbs wife grew into the kind of wife whose value was beyond measure. She developed into the kind of wife who was a treasure and a rare find, the kind of wife that shines. As she yielded herself to the Lord and His plan for her as a wife, she grew and developed. It was a process. She was willing. Not only was she willing, but she grabbed hold of how great, how vital, and how valuable her role as a wife really was. She embraced it. She did not take for granted that God had chosen her for this role. Instead, she was thankful. She was honored, and therefore, she was passionate about every task. She grew and she excelled.

You, too, can grow and develop into a Proverbs 31 wife. You too can spring forth, increase, and excel. More than ever, we need role models in our culture and time. Will you be that godly role model to a generation of wives who may otherwise lose their way?

_____

_____

_____

_____

I have been married for _____ years.

Am I continually learning and growing? Am I a better wife today than I was last year and the year before?

_____

_____

_____

_____

Have I been living below God's standard? What must I do today to excel?

_____

_____

_____

_____

Prayer

Lord, develop in me a virtuous and noble character, a character that is steadfast and pleasing to You. I choose to live according to Your holy standards. As I follow Your principles and Your ways, begin to increase and perfect my faith, my attitude, my actions, my gifts, and my skills that are necessary in building a godly marriage and home. Increase and perfect the love that I have in my heart for my husband. I don't want to be a common wife with a common marriage. I want more. I want to become a Proverbs 31 kind of wife. Help me to become a wife who is distinguishable and a wife that excels.

PERSONAL REFLECTIONS

_____

_____

_____

_____

_____

_____

_____

_____

_____

_____

_____

_____

_____

_____

_____

Day 30

I Am Submitting to the Process

A capable, intelligent, and virtuous woman—who is he who can find her?
She is far more precious than jewels and her value is above rubies or pearls.

Proverbs 31:10 AMP

Yesterday, we discovered that the Proverbs 31 wife was distinguishable and shined! I think it is safe to assume that she didn't just come into the world that way. Neither did she enter into her marriage from day one as a wife that had it all together. Even if she was a God-seeking, God-fearing, virtuous woman before she became a wife, how many of you know that marriage is brand new territory? She may have been experienced and skilled in many areas, but this was a brand new venture where new skills needed to be learned and mastered. Most likely she did not enter into the role of a wife as the praiseworthy and sought-after model we read about today. No. There was a process involved.

Nevertheless, she submitted herself to that process and in time, she became the kind of wife whose value is compared to that of jewels: rubies, pearls, and even diamonds in some translations. Did you know that there is a process a jewel undergoes in order to bring forth great value?

Beautiful jewels are created and formed deep under the surface of the earth, under great pressure and intense heat. The greater the pressure, the more beautiful the stone. The more intense the heat, the richer and truer the color.

When they are mined, most natural gemstones have a rough surface and an irregular shape. A skilled craftsman takes these stones from their raw state and cuts and polishes them to increase their beauty. He may even treat a stone with more heat to bring out an even deeper and richer color. The craftsman cuts the gems by grinding away materials until the desired shape is reached. The stones are then cut or faceted in such a way as to show off their unique characteristics. The purpose of the faceting is to allow as much light as possible to pass through it and reflect back to the viewer's eye. The work of the master cutter is to cut the stone in such a way as to permit the maximum amount of light to be reflected through it. It is cut in a way that shows off its color, its brilliance, its fire, and its sparkle to the best degree possible. The more facets, the more brilliance. These valuable beauties have been refined and cut to form.

A ruby is the most desired gem due to its rarity. The very thing that distinguishes a precious stone from what is considered a semi-precious stone is the stone's rarity. There are fewer to be found. Naturally, a rare stone will be more valuable. A ruby's hardness also makes it a desirable gem. It is tough and durable. The only natural stone harder than a ruby is a diamond.

Diamonds can only form under certain conditions. They are developed under pressure and high temperatures. Sometimes diamonds are brought to the surface by volcanic activity. It is said that 80 percent of all diamonds that are mined are not even suited for jewelry. We know that a diamond is the hardest and most durable of all stones. A diamond has to be cut and faceted as well, but it can only be cut by another diamond. No other natural mineral can even scratch it, and that is why diamonds can maintain their integrity for years and years. As a diamond's durability increases, so does its value. A diamond can dig through rock and polish other extremely hard minerals and metals. It is the only mineral that can do this and that increases its value. Other factors increase its value as well. Clarity is one of those factors. Clarity describes its purity. The clearer the diamond, the more valuable. With fewer imperfections and flaws, the diamond is considered rare and brings a high price.

The Amplified version of Proverbs 31:10 also mentions pearls. Pearls undergo a very interesting process as well. A pearl is formed inside the shell of a mollusk. An intruder, such as a grain of sand, gets inside the mollusk. It is actually very painful to that mollusk. The mollusk begins to secrete a substance called *nacre* to soothe the pain. The nacre covers the irritant and over a period of time, it builds layer upon layer until a remarkably beautiful pearl develops and comes forth. Pearls are soft, and absorb light as well as reflect it.

There is a process in which jewels come through which cause them to become the rare and valuable beauties that they are. The process takes time. The process is also strikingly similar to the process in which we ourselves often come through in order to grow, develop, mature, and become more like Christ. 1 Peter 2:5 says that we are "like living stones" being built into a spiritual house. God desires to develop something so precious, so beautiful, and so valuable within us. Because the process can be painful, not many will fully submit to it.

A Proverbs wife is far more precious than jewels, and her value is above rubies, diamonds, and pearls. Proverbs 31:10 leads us to believe that a virtuous wife, a wife of valor, is hard to find. It seems that even today, virtuous women are becoming rare. There are fewer and fewer who will maintain a standard of purity and holiness. There is a shortage of godly wives whom we can look to as role models. What about you? Will you allow God to refine you? Will you allow the Master craftsman to finish His work? Will you allow Him to grow you and develop you into a Proverbs 31 wife?

_____

_____

And I am convinced and sure of this very thing, that He Who began a good work in you will continue until the day of Jesus Christ [right up to the time of His return], developing [that good work] and perfecting and bringing it to full completion in you. (Philippians 1:6 AMP)

Though there may be pain in the process, am I willing to go through it?

_____

_____

_____

_____

Can I honestly say these words in my heart today, "I have no other will but Your will, Lord."

_____

_____

_____

_____

Prayer

Though I may encounter seasons where I am dealing with pressures of various kinds, I will allow You to produce in me something of great value, Lord. Though there may be days when the heat is on, I will allow You to bring forth my true colors and change in me anything that needs changing. I will allow You to cut away anything that would hinder me from becoming the unique and rare beauty that You have created me to be. Though there may be pain in the process, I trust in the Lord God my healer and the One who can take great pain and turn it into great purpose. Create in me a pure heart, O God, and renew a right spirit within me. Polish me until I truly reflect Your light. Have Your way in my life, Lord. I am submitting to the Process.

PERSONAL REFLECTIONS

_____

_____

_____

_____

_____

_____

_____

_____

_____

_____

_____

_____

_____

_____

_____

_____

_____

_____

_____

_____

_____

_____

_____

_____

_____

_____

_____

_____

_____

_____

_____

_____

Day 31

I Face the Future
With a Smile

For I know the plans I have for you," says the LORD. "They are plans for good and not for disaster, to give you a future and a hope.

Jeremiah 29:11 NLT

Dear woman of God, I do not know what you have been walking through in your own marriage, but I do know that there is hope for the future. As you commit your marriage and your home to the Lord, You can trust Him to keep it.

> For I know whom I have believed and am persuaded that He
> is able to keep what I have committed to him until that day.
> (2 Timothy 1:12b NKJV)

You are on a journey. Your relationship with the Lord is real. He knows you and you know Him. He knows your heart. He hears your prayers. You have chosen to trust Him. You have made a commitment to allow the Lord to shape you into the wife that He has called you to be. You have committed your husband and your marriage to God. And He is able to guard and keep that which you have committed to Him.

Furthermore, He sees you, your circumstances, where you've been, and where you are right now. He knows where you are headed! He has seen it all. He has seen it from beginning to end. He knows the plans that He has for you. They are good plans and you can face the future with a smile.

The Proverbs 31 wife was confident that the days ahead were bright. Proverbs 31:25 tells us that she rejoiced about the future.

> She shall rejoice in time to come. (Proverbs 31:25b NKJV)

The word rejoice here is the Hebrew word *sâchaq,* and it translates "to laugh in pleasure and to make merry." The Proverbs wife can smile and even laugh when she looks upon the days ahead. She actually looks forward to the future with confidence and gladness. Her confidence is in the Lord. She can trust that He is at work and that the future *is* bright. She is not worried or fearful about anything.

She has been sowing and planting. She has been watering and nurturing her marriage relationship. She can be sure that she will reap in time to come. Sowing is hard work. It comes with sweat and sometimes tears, but don't you know that the Psalmist assured us that those who sow in tears shall reap in joy!

> They who sow in tears shall reap in joy. (Psalm 126:5 NKJV)

The word for joy that I am referring to from Psalm 126:5 is the original Hebrew word *rinnâh.* It translates "rejoicing." If you have sown tears, get ready to reap joy. Like the Proverbs 31 wife, you too can rejoice and laugh with pleasure in time to come. This *rinnâh* kind of joy also means "gladness, shouts of joy, and **to triumph.**"

> And now, GOD, do it again—bring rains to our drought-stricken lives so those who planted their crops in despair will shout hurrahs at the harvest, so those who went off with heavy hearts will come home laughing, with armloads of blessing. (Psalm 126:5-6 MSG)

The Proverbs 31 wife can look well on the future. She is not anxious about it. She laughs without fear of the future. Her position is strong and secure. She has a positive outlook on the days ahead. She always faces tomorrow with a smile.

We are told in Genesis 8:22 that as long as the earth remains, seedtime *and* harvest shall not cease. Don't be deceived into thinking that all you have invested into the building of your marriage and home has amounted to nothing.

> Do not be deceived: God cannot be mocked. A man reaps what he sows. Whoever sows to please their flesh, from the flesh will reap destruction; whoever sows to please the Spirit, from the Spirit will reap eternal life. Let us not become weary in doing good, for at the proper time we will reap a harvest if we do not give up. (Galatians 6:7-9 NIV)

Galatians 6:7 insists that you will reap whatever you sow. Harvest time is coming! Verse nine goes on to encourage us to not grow weary of the sowing of good things, because in due season we will reap if we do not give up.

Ecclesiastes chapter 3 reminds us that "to everything there is a season; a season to plant and a season to reap… a season to heal and a season to build." Continue to sow. Continue to heal. Continue to build, and you too can look upon the future with confidence and joy. It's going to be worth it! You *will* triumph.

The Proverbs 31 wife honors her marriage. She recognizes the value of her role as a wife and is ready to fulfill it. Her desire is to help that man fulfill his God-given purposes—all that he has been called to be and to do. She has been pursuing godliness and lives according to a high moral standard. God has been developing her through every difficulty that she has faced. An inner strength of mind and spirit has grown on the inside. She is full of purpose as she builds her home. To the best of her abilities, she has become a good manager and steward of all that the Lord has given her.

Not only has she taken care of her family's physical needs, but she has also been dedicated to their spiritual well-being. She has found contentment within the field that the Lord has given her, and it has ₑat gain to her. She has been her husband's encourager. She edifies him and builds him up, and she has made him her priority. She does not hinder her husband in any way as he grows into his leadership role in their home. In these ways, she has truly contributed to bringing him into his full potential.

As a godly wife, she has demonstrated respect toward her husband, both privately and publically. This woman has made herself one with him, coming under one common mission. She adapts to her husband, and incredibly, she is able to adapt to every wind of change that has blown into their lives. This woman is unshakable and her marriage stronger than ever. She has truly clothed herself with strength and dignity.

The Proverbs 31 kind of wife has come to honor, regard, and deeply care for her husband by holding fast to her commitment of love. Her heart desires to have a marriage that truly reflects the love of Christ for His church and God honors that. She follows Christ's example in the way she lavishes her love upon her husband. She loves him with an unrelenting, unconditional love. Walking in forgiveness has become a lifestyle for her. Keeping her heart clear and handling conflict correctly, she has dressed herself in the wardrobe of love, the wardrobe that God has picked out for her. She is consistently growing and developing as a virtuous wife. She has become her husband's honor, his crown, his glory, and his trophy. She is a woman who fears the Lord. Her identity is in Christ and His plan and purpose for her. God has given her all things pertaining to life and godliness; therefore, she can do all things through Christ who strengthens her. She is completely capable of finishing her course. She is blessed. She is a blessing, and most certainly, she can look forward to a blessed future!

> So let's not allow ourselves to get fatigued doing good. At the right time we will harvest a good crop if we don't give up, or quit. Right now, therefore, every time we get the chance, let us work for the benefit of all, starting with the people closest to us...(Galatians 6:9-10 MSG)

Are you more determined to than ever to walk in your God-given role?

_____

_____

_____

_____

Will you take the very things that the Lord has spoken to your heart about in the last 31 days and apply them each day from this day forward?

_____

_____

_____

_____

Will you continue moving forward on the path to becoming the wife that God has created you to be?

_____

_____

_____

_____

Prayer

Lord, You are good and Your mercies are new every morning. Surely Your plans for me are good plans. I trust You with my life. I have committed every area of it to You, including my marriage. I move forward with great anticipation of all the things that You have in store. I am in great expectation of a blessed future. I rejoice in the days to come. Gladness fills my heart even now. Shouts of joy come forth from my mouth. A fresh new excitement is stirring within my inner being.

My position is strong and secure. Every good thing that I have sown is producing a harvest for me even now. I face the future with a smile.

PERSONAL REFLECTIONS

_____

_____

_____

_____

_____

_____

_____

_____

_____

_____

_____

_____

_____

_____

_____

Stay On Course

I want to encourage you to stay on course with your journey of growing in your marriage. Before we close this book, let's take a look at 1 Corinthians chapter 13 (MSG):

The Way of Love

If I speak with human eloquence and angelic ecstasy but don't love, I'm nothing but the creaking of a rusty gate. If I speak God's Word with power, revealing all his mysteries and making everything plain as day, and if I have faith that says to a mountain, "Jump," and it jumps, but I don't love, I'm nothing. If I give everything I own to the poor and even go to the stake to be burned as a martyr, but I don't love, I've gotten nowhere. So, no matter what I say, what I believe, and what I do, I'm bankrupt without love.

Love never gives up. Love cares more for others than for self. Love doesn't want what it doesn't have. Love doesn't strut, doesn't have a swelled head, doesn't force itself on others, isn't always "me first," doesn't fly off the handle, doesn't keep score of the sins of others, doesn't revel when others grovel, takes pleasure in the flowering of truth, puts up with anything, trusts God always, always looks for the best, never looks back, but keeps going to the end.

Love never dies. Inspired speech will be over some day; praying in tongues will end; understanding will reach its limit. We know only a portion of the truth, and what we say about God is always incomplete. But when the Complete arrives, our incompletes will be canceled. When I was an infant at my mother's breast, I gurgled and cooed like any infant. When I grew up, I left those infant ways for good.

We don't yet see things clearly. We're squinting in a fog, peering through a mist. But it won't be long before the weather clears and the sun shines bright! We'll see it all then, see it all as clearly as God sees us, knowing him directly just as he knows us! But for right now, until that completeness, we have three things to do to lead us toward that consummation: Trust steadily in God, hope unswervingly, love extravagantly. And the best of the three is love.

What beautiful scriptures concerning love! First Corinthians 13 is often referred to as the love chapter. I know…these are very familiar scriptures. They are so familiar that I presented them from the Message Bible to begin with, for the sake of getting a fresh new look at the love chapter and applying this *way of love* to our marriages.

My husband and I got married on November 4, 1988, and I was a brand new Christian. I gave my heart to the Lord the previous August, just three months before I would give my heart fully to my husband as his wife. I loved the Lord. I was one of those who had a radical conversion, if you know what I mean. Thank God we were both saved when we said, "I do." Our heart's desire was to put God at the center of our marriage. God honored that, and we both began to grow as a husband and wife.

I made my husband a special wedding gift and presented it to him on our wedding day. In calligraphy, I beautifully wrote 1 Corinthians 13 on a piece of fine parchment paper and burned the edges of the paper in the shape of a heart. I put a lot of time into it. I was proud of the framed finished product. It revealed my heart's desire and commitment to love him the way God wanted me to love him. Little did I know that I would spend the next twenty-seven years (and counting) learning just how to do that. I was just twenty-two years old, and I thought that I knew what real love was really all about. Please stop laughing so loud…so did you.

Let's take a closer look at those beautiful scriptures that I had penned on parchment from all the sincerity of my heart.

The chapter begins by communicating to us the truth that you can actually receive, operate in, and arrive at great levels in your Christianity, even exercising great acts of service and charity, *but if you don't have love, you really have nothing of value.* It profits you in no way. You are nothing special and you gain nothing by it.

Many times we seek to grow in our Christian walk with the Lord and in doing so, we mature in many ways. We serve God in our churches. We become leaders in many areas and take opportunities to be great influences to those around us. We can, however, do these very things while neglecting to demonstrate love toward our own spouse. Oh, it never starts out that way. The truth is, however, that love can be the hardest to demonstrate in our very own homes, behind closed doors, where we encounter tests on a daily basis. It is the place where we are most challenged. It is also the place that is most dear to us. There is really nothing more important to us than our own husband and children, our own family, our own home. It is the place where our testimony begins. We must first cultivate love there and let that love flow out to the world around us. It is a love that must be maintained and protected. If someone tells you that love doesn't take work or that marriage shouldn't require effort, they are not telling you the truth. Sometimes effort is required.

When I was a young wife with one toddler and a baby, I had a wonderful couple mentor me for a time. They mentored all the young married couples at the church we were a part of during those years. They were a great testimony before all of us. This couple had five children at the time. I say "at the time" because they went on to have four more. They loved the Lord. They were deeply in love with each other. Their children were all very well behaved. Their home was in order. They were servants and leaders in the house of God. They were servants and leaders in the community and had great influence everywhere with all people. And their secret to having a successful, loving marriage and home was this: dying to self. They would share with us the truth that when they got married, they had to die to self. With the raising of each child that the Lord blessed them with, they learned to die to self a little more. I heard their message loud and clear. I also have had many, many, opportunities to learn firsthand this principle of dying to self. It is the way of love.

Within the verses of 1 Corinthians 13, I see fourteen descriptions of what love really is (and isn't).

Number 1: *Love suffers long* (verse 4, NKJV)

I don't like to suffer. How could I have missed that as I penned my beautiful wedding gift to Gary? Surely I must have been focused entirely upon perfecting my calligraphic lettering on that one. Other versions use the words "love is patient." Yes, that was the version that I copied. That is how I missed the suffering part...and suffering long, besides!

Matthew Henry says this about longsuffering: "It can endure evil, injury, and provocation, without being filled with resentment, indignation, or revenge. It makes the mind firm, gives it power over the angry passions, and furnishes it with a persevering patience, that shall rather wait and wish for the reformation of a brother than fly out in resentment of his conduct. It will put up with many slights and neglects from the person it loves, and wait long to see the kindly effects of such patience on him."

John Wesley describes love that suffers long in this way: "It inspires the sufferer at once with the most amiable sweetness, and the most fervent and tender affection."

Albert Barnes defines suffering long like this: "...slowness to anger or passion; longsuffering, patient endurance, forbearance. It is opposed to haste; to passionate expressions and thoughts, and to irritability. It denotes the state of mind which can bear long when oppressed, provoked, calumniated, and when one seeks to injure us."

"Suffereth long" in the Greek actually translates "to be long spirited and to patiently endure." Ah, those terms might better describe me *now*, but they didn't exactly describe me in my twenties. Patience and endurance is developed over time. In fact, all of the following descriptions of love are developed as we grow. Verse 11 talks about that very thing.

> When I was a child, I talked like a child, I thought like a child,
> I reasoned like a child; now that I have become a man, I am
> done with childish ways and have put them aside.
> (1 Corinthians 13:11 AMPC)

Children throw temper tantrums. They pout when they do not get their own way. They withhold affection when they are angry. Children are by nature very demanding. This scripture, however, is not referring to an infant or a minor. The word for childish in verse 11 is the Greek word *nēpios*, referring to an immature Christian. A Christian who grows and matures puts away or puts aside the immature things: immature speech, immature thinking, and immature reasoning or understanding. If we put all those immature things away, being done with them, we will cease from behaving like a child. After all, we are to "grow up in all things into Him who is the head—Christ." (Ephesians 4:15)

Number 2: *Love* suffers long and *is kind* (verse 4, NKJV)

I like what the Expositor's Bible Commentary has to say about this. "Love suffereth long, and is kind"; it reveals itself in a magnanimous bearing of injuries and in a considerate and tender imparting of benefits. It returns good for evil; not readily provoked by slights and wrongs, it ever seeks to spend itself in kindnesses."

I want to be the kind of person who ever seeks to spend myself in kindness and not just when someone is kind and loving to me, but even when they are not. And I want to be the kind of wife who ever seeks to spend myself in kindness toward my husband, when he is kind to me and even when he is not…

Matthew 5:46-48 (MSG) says, "If all you do is love the lovable, do you expect a bonus? Anybody can do that. If you simply say hello to those who greet you, do you expect a medal? Any run-of-the-mill sinner does that. In a word, what I'm saying is, Grow up. You're kingdom subjects. Now live like it. Live out your God-created identity. Live generously and graciously toward others, the way God lives toward you."

Can I be kind and loving even when someone else is being unkind and mean? Am I capable of doing the hard thing, or do I only look to do what is easy?

And here are the rest of love's characteristics…

Number 3: *Love does not envy* **(NKJV)**

It doesn't boil over with jealousy (AMP)

Number 4: *Love is not puffed up* **(NKJV)**

It does not boast (NIV)
It is not conceited (arrogant and inflated with pride) – AMP

Number 5: *Love does not behave or act unbecomingly*

It is not rude (AMP)
Love does not dishonor others (NIV)

Number 6: *Love is not self-seeking* **(NIV)**

It does not insist on its own rights or its own way (AMP)

This is the "dying to self" part. I call it the "what about me, me, me syndrome."

Number 7: *Love is not easily angered* **(NIV)**

Love does not fly off the handle (MSG)

Love is not irritable (ESV)

Love is not touchy, fretful, or resentful (AMP)

Number 8: *Love keeps no record of wrong* (NIV)

Does not keep score of the sins of others (MSG)

It takes no account of the evil done to it [pays no attention to a suffered wrong] AMP

Number 9: *Love does not rejoice at wrongdoing, but rejoices with the truth* (ESV)

Number 10: *Love bears all things* (NKJV)

This phrase "bears all things" translates "to roof over or to cover with silence." The NIV uses the words "always protects." To cover with silence is an interesting translation. Bearing all things requires a level of maturity that includes knowing when to keep our mouths closed and when to be quiet. Can I bear all things in a quiet manner that will prove to protect our love relationship? The Amplified Bible uses the words, "love bears up under anything and everything that comes." These are powerful words...

Number 11: *Always trusts* (NIV)

Is ever ready to believe the best in every person (AMP)

Number 12: *Love always hopes* (NIV)

Its hopes are fadeless under all circumstances (AMP)

Number 13: *Love endureth all things* (KJV)

Love endures everything [without weakening] (AMP)

Endureth translates "to stay under, remain, undergo, bear trials, have fortitude, abide, tarry and to be patient." The ESV uses the words, "Love *always* perseveres."

And finally...

Number 14: *Love never fails* (KJV)

The word "fails" is the Greek word *ekpipto* translating "to become inefficient, takes no effect, fades out, to drop away, or **to be driven off one's course.**"

LOVE will not be driven off course.

I hope that all of these principles were covered in some way during the last thirty-one days. I know...every one of them is challenging. As I said from the beginning, learning to love is a process. In respect to loving our husbands and fulfilling the role that the Lord has given us as wives, we must be *determined* to get on course, the course that the Lord has laid out for us to follow. And if, by some set of circumstances, we find that we have slipped off course, we can get right back on track. We don't give up, but we begin again. The Lord will help us! He has given us the ability to become all that He has called us to be as wives. In closing, I invite you to make this declaration and promise with me today:

"I WILL NOT BE DRIVEN OFF COURSE."

– JENNIFER RASH

Notes

Introduction; Marriage is Honorable

1. Strong's Hebrew and Greek Dictionary, Strong's #G5093; honourable
2. http://dictionary.reference.com/browse/honorable

Day 1: I am His Suitable Helper

1. Strong's Hebrew and Greek Dictionary, Strong's #H2896; Good
2. Strong's Hebrew and Greek Dictionary, Strong's #H5828; Help Meet
3. Brown-Driver-Briggs' Hebrew Definitions, #H5828; Help Meet

Day 3: I am a Devoted Wife

1. Brown-Driver-Briggs' Hebrew Definitions, #H2896; Good

Day 4: I am the Builder of My House

1. Brown-Diver-Brigg's Hebrew Definitions, #H7451; Evil
2. Strong's Hebrew and Greek Dictionary, Strong's #H7451; Evil
3. Strong's Hebrew and Greek Dictionary, Strong's #H2040; Plucketh it down
4. Strong's Hebrew and Greek Dictionary, Strong's #H1129; Buildeth

Day 6: I Find Great Satisfaction in Building My Home

1. Thayer's Greek Definitions, #G841; Contentment

Day 9: I am Under the Same Mission as My Husband

1. http://www.biblestudytools.com/dictionaries/bakers-evangelical-dictionary/authority.html; definition of authority

Day 11: I Follow My Husband's Guidance

1. Strong's Hebrew and Greek Dictionary, Strong's #5293; Obedient
2. Thayer's Greek Definitions, #5293; Obedient

Day 12: I am One with My Husband

1. Strong's Hebrew and Greek Dictionary, Strong's #4347; Joined
2. Scripture: Mark 10:9 King James Version (KJV)
3. Strong's Hebrew and Greek Dictionary, Strong's #G4801: Joined together
4. HelpsBible.com; yoke
5. Scripture: Genesis 2:24King James Version (KJV)

6. Strong's Hebrew and Greek Dictionary, Strong's #H1692; Cleave
7. Brown-Driver-Briggs' Hebrew Definitions, #H1692; Cleave
8. Scripture: Mark 3:25New King James Version (NKJV)
9. Kingdom Dynamics, Male and Female, God's Image Bearers in the Earth,Jack Hayford, New Spirit Filled Life Bible, page 5, Thomas
10. Nelson, Inc., 2002

Day 14: I Follow Christ's Example in the Way that I Love

1. Merriam-Webster Dictionary; Lavish
2. Scripture; Romans 8:38-39 MSG
3. Samuele Bacchiocchi, *The Marriage Covenant.* Biblical Perspectives, 1991.

Day 15: My Marriage is Holy

1. Baker's Evangelical Dictionary of Biblical Theology - Covenant
2. http://www.biblestudytools.com/dictionary/covenant/
3. Steps of Ancient Covenant Making, Session 2, http://www.thectp.org/notes/inheritance/inheritance_2.pdf

Day 16: I Am a Covenant Keeper

1. The Marriage Covenant, Samuele Bacchiocchi, Chapters 1 and 2
2. https://www.biblicalperspectives.com/books/marriage/1.html
3. Jesus the Bridegroom, Brant Pitre

Day 17: I Keep My Heart Clear

1. Strong's Hebrew and Greek Dictionary, #G48; Purified
2. Scripture; John 8:44 NKJV
3. Strong's Hebrew and Greek Dictionary, #G505; Unfeigned (Sincere)
4. Strong's Hebrew and Greek Dictionary, #G1619; Fervently
5. Strong's Hebrew and Greek Dictionary, #G5483; Forgive
6. Quote on Forgiveness; Raleigh B. Washington
7. New Spirit Filled Life Bible, 2002; Kingdom Dynamics note page 1675

Day 18: I Handle Conflict Correctly

1. Strong's Hebrew and Greek Dictionary, #G2127; Blessing

Day 19: I am My Husband's Crown

1. Strong's Hebrew and Greek Dictionary, #H2428; Virtuous (Excellent)
2. Strong's Hebrew and Greek Dictionary, H7919; Prudent
3. Strong's Hebrew and Greek Dictionary, G987; Blasphemed

Day 20: I am My Husband's Glory

    1. Strong's Hebrew and Greek Dictionary, #G1391; Glory
    2. Thayer's Greek Definitions, #G1391; Glory

Day 21: I am a Trophy Wife

    1. Strong's Hebrew and Greek Dictionary, #G2272; Quiet

Day 22: I am Strong and Graceful

    1. Strong's Hebrew and Greek Dictionary, #H5797; Strength
    2. Strong's Hebrew and Greek Dictionary, #H553; Strengthens
    3. Scripture:

Day 23: The Fear of the Lord; hebrew4christians.com, John J. Parsons

Day 24: I am Blessed

    1. Strong's Hebrew and Greek Dictionary, #H833; Blessed
    2. Brown-Driver-Briggs' Hebrew Definitions, #H833; Blessed
    3. Strong's Hebrew and Greek Dictionary, #G2137; Prosper

Day 25: Name of Chapter

    1. Strong's Hebrew and Greek Dictionary, #H6509; Fruitful
    2. Strong's Hebrew and Greek Dictionary, #H1612; Vine

Day 27: My Oil Keeps Burning

    1. Strong's Hebrew and Greek Dictionary, #H3915, Night

Day 28: My Lamp Stays Lit

    1. Parable of the Wise and Foolish Virgins; Matthew 25:1-13

Day 29: I Excel

    1. Brown-Driver-Briggs' Hebrew Definitions, #H5927; Excellest (Excel)
    2. Strong's Hebrew and Greek Dictionary, #H5927; Excellest (Excel)

Day 31: I Face the Future with a Smile

    1. Strong's Hebrew and Greek Dictionary, #H7832; Rejoice
    2. Strong's Hebrew and Greek Dictionary, #H7440; Joy

3. Proverbs 31:25 Expanded Bible, NLT, AMP, MSG
4. She is strong and is respected by the people [^LStrength and dignity/honor are her clothing].She ·looks forward to the future with joy [^Llaughs at the future; ^Cshe is not anxious].

   She is clothed with strength and dignity, and she laughs without fear of the future.

   Strength and dignity are her clothing *and* her position is strong and secure; she rejoices over the future [the latter day or time to come, knowing that she and her family are in readiness for it]!

   Her clothes are well-made and elegant, and she always faces tomorrow with a smile.

5. Ecclesiastes 3:1-3 NKJV

Closing Chapter: Stay on Course

1. Matthew Henry's Commentary on the Whole Bible; 1 Corinthians 13:4
2. John Wesley's Explanatory Notes; 1 Corinthians 13:4
3. Albert Barnes' Notes on the Bible; 1 Corinthians 13:4#G3114; Suffereth long
4. Thayer's Greek Definitions, #G3114; Suffereth long
5. Strong's Hebrew and Greek Dictionary, #G3516; Child
6. Strong's Hebrew and Greek Dictionary, #G4722; Beareth
7. Strong's Hebrew and Greek Dictionary, #G1601; Fails

About the Author

Jennifer Rash is a wife and mother of three boys ages 26, 24, and 16. She resides in South Carolina where she and her husband pastor City of Hope Church in Spartanburg, South Carolina. Jennifer is an ordained minister and has a heart for women's ministry, leading women's conferences, Bible studies, women's groups, and mentoring young women. She formerly served as Women's Ministry Director for the northern section of South Carolina under the Women's Ministries of the Assemblies of God. She has also served as the Intercessory Prayer Director for the South Carolina district of the Women's Ministries of the Assemblies of God, upholding its leaders through prayer and leading Prayer Summits across the state. She has traveled all over South Carolina, speaking to women's groups and pouring into women of all walks of life. Currently she leads the Praise and Coffee group of Spartanburg, South Carolina, and is co-pastor with her husband of twenty-seven years.